Waiting for the Sky to Fall

Jacqueline Wilson

Waiting for the Sky to Fall

Oxford University Press 1983
Oxford   Toronto   Melbourne

Oxford University Press, Walton Street, Oxford OX2 6DP

Oxford London Glasgow
New York Toronto Melbourne Auckland
Kuala Lumpur Singapore Hong Kong Tokyo
Delhi Bombay Calcutta Madras Karachi
Nairobi Dar es Salaam Cape Town

and associated companies in
Beirut Berlin Ibadan Mexico City Nicosia

Oxford is a trade mark of Oxford University Press

© Jacqueline Wilson 1983
First published 1983

British Library Cataloguing in Publication Data

Wilson, Jacqueline
Waiting for the sky to fall.
I. Title
823'.914[J]   PZ7
ISBN 0-19-271485-6

Photoset by Rowland Phototypesetting Ltd
Bury St Edmunds, Suffolk
Printed by Biddles & Co Ltd
Guildford, Surrey

Chapter 1

I peered at my ancient Magic Roundabout alarm clock. Dougal's tail wagged backwards and forwards in time to the ticking. It must ache unbearably, wagging once a second all through the day, all through the night. It was only just gone five. I'd woken even earlier this morning. I knew I wouldn't be able to go back to sleep.

Exam questions ricocheted through my head. I groaned and put my hands over my ears, although there was no way of muffling them. I tried humming dementedly, and then stopped because Nicola was stirring and I didn't want to wake her up.

I was clutching my ears so tightly that they started throbbing. When I took my hands away for a moment's relief I was distracted by the birds singing surprisingly loudly outside the window. I'd no idea that Waverton Shopping Parade had its own dawn chorus. It sounded like the countryside. If I drew the limp curtains perhaps I'd see lush green fields and shady woods and far-off misty mountains instead of ugly main road and the Wavy Line Grocer, the Off-Licence and the Clean-Kwick Dry Cleaners.

It was the sort of pretend game I'd often played with Nicola.

'Pretend we can magic ten new outfits of clothes inside our wardrobe. What are you going to have?'

'Pretend we can wake up completely different people. Who are you going to be?'

'Pretend my glass snowstorm is a crystal ball. Let's stare into it and predict our future.'

I sat up in bed and reached for the snowstorm. It wasn't really glass. It was plastic, and the little house and the fir trees and the tiny reindeer were plastic too. Some of the so-called snow seemed to have seeped out in a mysterious way, because there wasn't a satisfactory snowstorm any more even when I shook it violently. A few specks drifted here and there, but the house and the fir trees and the reindeer remained clearly visible.

I'd had it ten years, since I was five. I'd been given it as a going-home present at my first proper party. Nicola hadn't been invited and was very envious, even though she didn't really know much about parties. I came home and showed off determinedly about the lovely time I'd had, although I'd actually been miserable. I was dressed in my ordinary every-day frock, but all the other girls had the long party dresses fashionable at that time. I'd helped myself to two marmite sandwiches thinking they were chocolate spread and had got an awful shock. I was scared to leave anything on my plate so I spent half an hour chewing minute bites while everyone else grabbed sausages on sticks and crisps. We had games after tea and I began to enjoy myself at last because I kept winning, but after I'd been given two prize balloons the Mother and the Auntie deliberately ignored me and let some of the other children win. I tried not to let them see I cared, but my eyes itched with tears. I was starting to worry about going home time too. Mum was coming to fetch me. I'd seen children smirking when they looked at her. She was so terribly fat, an outsize human version of the wobbly pink milk jelly we'd had at tea.

She was the first mother to arrive. I wanted to hide behind an armchair and pretend she was nothing to do with me, but when I heard someone whispering Fatchops I wanted to rush up to Mum and put my arms round her. I didn't do either. I thanked the Mother and Auntie for the lovely party, my voice croaky with embarrassment, and they gave me false smiles, my two prize balloons – and the snowstorm as a going-home present.

When I got home I was quite happy to give one of the balloons to Nicola. Mum suggested it would be kind to give her the snowstorm too, as I had been enjoying so many treats at the party, but I hung on to it determinedly. I let Nicola shake it occasionally and I made up stories for her about the tiny people who lived in the little house and rode on the reindeer, but it was always *my* snowstorm. I once hit Nicola hard with it when

6

I caught her having a surreptitious shake withou‪
mission.

It seemed ludicrous now that I could have made suc
about a silly little plastic toy. I shook it again and stare‪
dandruffy flecks settling on the plastic thatch of the ho
only it was a crystal ball and I could tell if I still ha‪. ‪ne
glittering future Dad had planned for me.

He left me alone as a baby, but when I was about two I
startled him in the shop by pointing to all the different chocolate bars and telling him their names. I think I just recognised
their shape and colour, but Dad thought I was reading. He
decided to teach me to read some more, and bought me a
whole pile of Ladybird books. I was heartily sick of Jane and
Peter by the time I started at infant school, but I could read and
write fluently.

Dad read an article about gifted children, and decided I was
one. He made me sit a lot of tests and I tried hard to solve all the
silly puzzles to prove I was clever. I learnt that the best way to
impress him was to sit with my head in our jumble-sale set of
Arthur Mee's Children's Encyclopedia. I made my way
through all ten volumes but I didn't actually read much of
them. I pored over the colour plates instead and made up
imaginary games about the people in the pictures.

Dad decided that I wasn't learning enough at my school. He
said he didn't hold with all this free expression. He didn't see
the point of making castles out of toilet-rolls and egg boxes
and mucking about with little coloured rods. But when I was
ten I won a scholarship to Lady Margaret Lancaster's, a posh
public day-school in the next town. Everyone was at least a
year older than me in my class, and they giggled behind my
back because I was such a baby and I didn't talk in their
superior plummy way. Thank goodness Mum had to buy the
proper school uniform, so at least they couldn't sneer about
my clothes too.

I was at this strange, strict new school because I was gifted,
but at first I didn't feel it. Everyone else in the class knew lots of
French and English Grammar and Geography and History and
all different sorts of Maths. I hadn't learnt any of this at my old
school and felt horribly ignorant. I was given extra homework
and the teachers were kind and encouraging, but I felt stupid

7

and had nightmares for weeks. But by the end of the first term I'd more or less caught up, and by the end of the first year I came top in all the exams.

I came top year after year, although it began to be more and more of an effort. Before my mock O levels I revised until eleven or twelve at night, terrified that I wasn't remembering any of it. I was sick every single morning while I took the exams, but somehow I managed to get A grades in all eleven of them.

Everyone expected a repeat performance in my proper O levels (Oh God, oh God.) Then I was going to take three, maybe four A levels and try for Oxbridge when I was seventeen. Dad said I had to aim for the top. Then I'd stay on at university doing research and eventually become a professor. Professor Katherine Petworthy.

I probably wouldn't marry. Boys didn't seem to think much of me. I'd overheard two horrible spotty specimens discussing me in the shop. 'Don't reckon her, do you? Hair like a Brillo pad and she hasn't got any tits.' I nearly burst into tears, although I knew it was silly to care what idiots like that thought. But maybe I'd meet some sensitive and gentle man at university who would want me for my mind and not my body. We needn't get married. I certainly didn't want any children. I hated babies.

Nicola wanted us to share a flat together when we were grown-up but recently I'd started to think I'd sooner live on my own. I ought to earn a large salary as a Professor so I could probably afford a redbrick Victorian villa with stained glass windows and William Morris wallpaper, or a tiny whitewashed cottage all hollyhocks and roses outside in the garden and inside on the chintz, or an elegant town flat with furniture as stark as modern sculpture.

I'd day-dreamed for hours, furnishing each fantasy house, imagining ornaments, pictures, even mundane things like saucepans. I tried to build them up in my mind now, but all I could see was the little plastic house trapped in its wispy snowstorm.

Maybe I wasn't going to have a glittering future after all. Maybe I was out of the race already because I'd fallen at the first real fence. Eleven huge, spiked fences: English Language,

English Literature, History, Geography, French, Latin, Greek, Maths, Biology, Physics and Chemistry. Even whispering the words made my tummy go hard and hot. I saw myself crashing into the fences, knocking them down like dominoes, and I clutched my ears and hummed again, trying to stop myself thinking.

I had to stop thinking about the exams. I'd taken them, it was all over. I mustn't think about that terrifying envelope arriving in August. I mustn't think about Dad and Miss Hyde and Mrs Philpotts and the sniggering, snobby girls in my class. I mustn't think, I mustn't think, I mustn't think.

I gabbled snatches of poems and plays, even nursery rhymes, names of magazines and chocolate bars, until I'd shaken up a snowstorm in my mind and obscured those awful O levels. I didn't need to think about them for weeks. I had nearly the whole of the summer holidays before the results. There was no point wasting all those wonderful weeks of freedom worrying. I didn't even have to go back to school until the end of the term now that I'd done my last O level, not to do lessons anyway. I had to start the silly Work Experience scheme next week, but that might be fun, especially as Miss Hyde said I could help her with some of the first formers. After that I'd be free.

I'd have to help out in the shop of course, but there should still be plenty of time for myself. I glanced guiltily at Nicola, huddled under her green candlewick with her shabby brood of animals. I knew she was counting on me doing all sorts of things with her. Bread and jam picnics in Richmond Park and Kew Gardens. Walks down by the river. Long browses in the library. And then there were the Paper People. I hadn't played the game with her for ages, because I'd been so busy swotting for O levels. I knew she was hoping we could have a really long session together this week-end. I used to enjoy the Paper People game just as much as she did, but now I felt ashamed of playing it.

Last term when I was alone with Miss Hyde and we were discussing the concept of childhood, I suddenly asked her if she thought it abnormal to play imaginary games at my age.

I blushed as I said it, feeling a fool, but Miss Hyde was comforting.

9

'You've read about Gondal and Angria, haven't you, Katherine? And it's not just the Brontës. Eleanor Farjeon used to play imaginary games with her brothers until they were well into their twenties. And hang on, there's a children's book by Antonia Forest, *Peter's Room*, I think it's in the library, where a whole group of imaginative and intelligent teenagers make up an elaborate fantasy game.'

The Paper People might just be counted an imaginative and intelligent elaborate fantasy game, and maybe some of the other games we used to play, like Black and White Island and the Revolving Castle, but there were many other games that Nicola and I played that were simply babyish and pathetic. Miss Hyde would hardly think me a brilliant little Brontë if she knew about the Hungry Harriet game, the Rude Word game, and Woffle, Sniffle and Muffle.

Sniffle's ears were poking out of Nicola's bedcovers and Woffle was lying right across her face, his fat tummy pressed against her nose. Muffle was doubtless lurking in her arms. They were three very elderly toy animals of indeterminate breed. Well, Sniffle was clearly a rabbit, though he'd become very long and limp through the years, and his back paws had been amputated in an accident we could now barely remember. Woffle was probably a koala bear, although his plush had once been an unlikely and brilliant turquoise and was now a dingy shade of sky. Muffle had never been intended as an animal of any species. He had been a terrible fake fur muff that Mum had made to match the collar on the coat I had to wear one everlasting embarrassing winter. One year later (there are two and a quarter years between us, but she is big and I am small) Nicola inherited the coat and muff and went through equal agonies, but eventually we both outgrew the outfit. When we no longer had to wear him, Muffle suddenly became interesting, a small, brown animal with a well-developed and endearing personality.

We used to share them out at bedtime, taking scrupuious turns. For the last few years I'd been happy to let them reside permanently in Nicola's bed but she still sometimes persuaded me to make them talk. It was ridiculous, great girls in their teens playing with nursery toys. If anyone ever found out they'd think me severely subnormal, not gifted.

I decided that I was going to have to be firm with Nicola this holiday. She would have to play these silly games by herself. She ought really to give them up too. We should try to make the effort to be like ordinary girls. Nicola was even more of a misfit at her school than I was at mine.

It was time I got rid of all my old toys and bits and pieces. It was the first thing I could do these holidays. I decided to make a proper list of tasks. I got up and started quietly searching for a piece of paper. I knew I could find any number of spare pages in my school exercise books, but I didn't want to go anywhere near the crammed satchel I'd hidden at the back of the wardrobe. If I looked at those pages of my neat, royal blue writing I'd start panicking again, and memories of the last three weeks would overwhelm me.

I ended up tearing out two pages from the middle of Nicola's school jotter. She turned over and muttered when the paper crackled, but luckily didn't wake up. I wondered if I'd be able to wheedle an exercise book out of Dad. He kept a stock of them in the shop, limp, uninspiring things with cheap, fuzzy paper, but he behaved as if they were medieval manuscripts whenever Nicola or I asked him for one.

'How can I possibly make a profit when you two are always at me demanding half the shop?' he'd bark. 'If you have a notebook you must pay for it, just like anyone else.'

He gave me fifty pence a week for pocket-money. Nicola only got forty pence. He often refused to give it to us too, because of some real or imagined misdemeanour. We were supposed to buy everything we needed with our pocket money – birthday presents, stamps, pens, pencils – and pay for all school donations and outings. We couldn't earn any extra money. Dad expected us to deliver papers every morning and help out in the shop after school and at week-ends for nothing.

It was rarely any use going to Mum for money. Her housekeeping allowance was so meagre she couldn't make ends meet herself. Whenever things got desperate and we couldn't afford something we *had* to buy, the three of us had to go to Dad and plead. I couldn't bear the look on his face at these times. How could he triumph at such a degrading victory? But

11

I was the best at getting round him, much better than Mum or poor old Nicola.

I got back into bed and started writing my list on my stolen piece of paper:

1. Clear out toys.

If Nicola couldn't be persuaded to put away childish things too, then perhaps she'd like to inherit mine. I could at long last give her the snowstorm. Although it was more an ornament than a toy. She wouldn't really want it now anyway. Maybe she'd like the doll's house I made out of cartons and cotton reels? (I'd enjoyed the egg-box era at my first school, even if it did infuriate my father). I'd spent one whole winter on the doll's house, upholstering the furniture with scraps of velvet, making little curtains and tapestry rugs, fashioning pots and pans and a tiny tea service out of some clay from school. Why hadn't I ever made a doll family to live in the elaborate little house? It would be easy enough. I could pinch a packet of pipe-cleaners from the shop, twist them into people, and flesh out their skeletons with pink cotton. Nicola might be able to make them, but they'd have to be nudists: she was hopeless at sewing. Perhaps I'd keep the doll's house until I'd made a decently clad family to live in it.

I didn't really have many toys left. Dad always said they were a waste of money and we'd be better off reading than mucking about with damn-daft toys. Perhaps it was time I threw out some of my books? Nicola had long ago inherited my baby books. I'd found out at Lady Margaret Lancaster's that I'd been reading the wrong books. I'd read early, I'd read omnivorously, but I'd somehow managed to miss all the established nursery classics. I was eleven before I caught up with Alice and Winnie-the-Pooh and Mole and Ratty and Toad. Privately I didn't feel I'd missed out on much. I'd been very happy with my cheap editions of Enid Blyton and my Stories for Girls omnibus and endless comics from the shop. My literary diet grew more nourishing when Dad started selling children's paperbacks, although I had to read each book very carefully, never opening them up properly, so that Dad could sell them afterwards. I deliberately broke the spine of *The Railway Chil-*

dren and *Little Women* so that I could keep them for myself. In both books the father was absent nearly all the time and the mothers were lovely.

Nicola had read them both several times already so she probably wouldn't want them, and she certainly wouldn't want any of the Penguins I'd been slowly collecting for myself over the last couple of years.

I crossed out the first and only resolution on my holiday list. I wondered what else to put. I ought to forget about Nesbit and Alcott and get to grips with my holiday reading. Miss Hyde had given me a long list, all my A level literature set books, some general reading that she suggested to the whole class, and a dozen extra books just for me because she felt I'd appreciate them.

Until I started the examination nightmare I'd been sure I'd appreciate them too. I'd got several of the books out of the library. I leant over and picked up *What Maisie Knew* because it was about a child. I tried reading the first page. My heart started thudding and I reread it. The sentences seemed perfectly sensible and yet I couldn't understand what was happening. I tried a third time, but by the time I'd got to the end of each sentence I'd forgotten what had happened at the beginning. My brain seemed to have solidified. I could almost feel it, a heavy monument to my own stupidity. But I wasn't stupid, I was gifted, I always came top, oh God, what was happening to me, why wouldn't the nightmare stop?

I threw the book on the floor and huddled under my bedcovers, trying to get back to sleep. I shut my eyes tight, but although I could blot out the early morning sunshine I couldn't even shade my terror. I started shivering with panic, and had to clutch myself tightly, my knees curled right up under my chin.

I lay until I heard Dad's alarm clock at six. I heard him groan irritably and then shuffle to the bathroom. After he'd dressed he went downstairs to start sorting the newspapers. Nicola and I didn't have to get up until half-past six, but I couldn't bear to stay in bed any longer.

I washed and pulled on a shirt and my one and only precious pair of jeans.

'I don't know why you wear those common things, like any

13

scruffy yob off the street,' Dad said as I went into the shop. It was his automatic response whenever he saw me wearing them. 'What are you doing up so early? Well, give us a hand, don't just stand there looking helpless, for Gawd's sake.'

I started sorting the papers too, glad to have something simple to concentrate on.

'Cat got your tongue?' Dad said sharply, but he glanced at me with concern. 'You look a bit seedy. Not sickening for anything, are you?'

'No. I just didn't sleep very well.'

'I don't know, there's always something the matter with you nowadays. If you're not being sick you've got a headache, and now you've started on this not sleeping caper. What's the matter with you?' He answered himself immediately. 'You're a bag of nerves, that's what it is. Look at you now, nibbling at your lip, twitching and fiddling, *stop* it! Don't jump like that.'

'Well, don't get on at me,' I said, and held my breath.

I could sometimes get away with answering him back, and my luck was in today.

'I'm worried about you, girl, can't you see?' said Dad. 'You look like a panda, white face, great bags under your eyes. Katherine? What *is* it?'

He stopped sorting the papers and stood peering at me. I didn't answer. He reached out and took hold of my arm, gently. It felt strange and awkward because we rarely touched.

'I'm worried about my O levels,' I whispered. 'I think I've failed them.'

I'd said it. I'd told him. I'd admitted it at last.

'Nonsense!' said Dad. 'What's really bothering you?'

'The exams,' I said.

'But there's nothing to worry about, you fool. They're over and done with. Look, are you helping me or not? The paper boys will be arriving in a minute.'

We both started sorting the papers again. My hands were so damp that my fingers became black with newsprint.

I tried for a third time.

'Dad, I really think I've mucked them up. It was so awful. I couldn't seem to think straight. I tried so hard, and yet – oh Dad, you won't hate me for ever if I've done badly, will you?'

'Stop being so bally dramatic. Who do you think you are,

Sarah Bernhardt? Don't be so daft. Of course you haven't done badly. You've never failed an exam in your life. Look at your Mocks. All A's. And that's what you'll get for your O levels, or I'll eat my hat.'

He really did own a hat, a terrible, sporty affair with a little feather at the side. He called it his Robin Hood and said he'd worn it in his 'courting' days. As far as I knew he'd never done any courting. He didn't even marry until he was forty-six. I couldn't help imagining him eating the hat after he'd read my results. I saw him munching doggedly at the dusty old material, choking on the feather. My lips trembled and I made a silly little snort, half sob, half snigger.

'That's it, cheer up for Gawd's sake. I've never known such a ninny. And don't rub your eyes like that, you've got newsprint all over your face. Where's your hankie? Strewth, you're hopeless.'

I knew it wasn't any use trying to tell him. He would only be convinced by the actual examination results. I continued to sort papers in silence, feeling sick.

I heard the alarm go off upstairs at half-past six, and a few minutes later Nicola came down into the shop.

'Why are you up so early, Kath?' she asked sleepily.

'Kath*erine*!' Dad shouted. 'Your mother and I took the trouble to give both of you pretty names. Why do you have to ruin them? And you could do with getting up early too, young lady. Look at you! Haven't you even washed? There's sleepy dust in your eyes, ugh, you disgust me. And that awful hair. Get it cut.'

Nicola ran her hand through her unkempt fringe. Her mouth puckered, the way it always did when she was frightened.

'Stop pulling that bloody silly face!' Dad raged. 'Why do you have to go round looking demented all the time? Tuck that blouse in properly, you sloppy little madam. You look hideous in that awful uniform. Come on, get cracking, get your newspapers together. Not those ones, oh Gawd, *look*, can't you?'

Nicola bent over the papers, screwing her face up. Even she realised it would make him worse if she cried.

I put my own newspapers into my canvas shoulder-bag and

15

we both went outside. Nicola leant against the wall, still fighting tears.

'Don't take any notice of him.'

'He said I – I disgust him,' Nicola said, and a tear spurted down her plump cheek.

'He didn't mean it. It's just his way. He was just as irritable with me.'

But we both knew there was a difference in the way Dad talked to us. He was grumpily affectionate with me. He was grumpily spiteful to Nicola.

'Come on. If we're late back he'll only moan more,' I said.

'He said I look hideous.'

'No he didn't. Only in your uniform. You know it irritates him. Oh Nic, you were the one that started him off, you know he goes spare if you call me Kath.'

'I can't remember all these things the way you can. And anyway, it doesn't work even if I do. He's always on at me, even if I haven't opened my mouth. You don't know how awful it is being me. I'd give anything to be you.'

'Don't be daft,' I snapped, just like Dad. Then I felt guilty. 'Hey, when you get home from school shall we play with the Paper People?'

'Oh yes!' said Nicola. 'Oh Kath, yes, let's! We haven't played for ages. Do you really mean it?'

I regretted saying it already but I couldn't go back on it now. It was worrying, having such power over Nicola. Her big, eager, shiny face irritated me.

'Yes, I really mean it. You ought to wash properly, you know. And if you'd only tie your hair up he wouldn't moan about it so much. Here, I've got a rubber band in my pocket.'

Nicola bent down gratefully while I scooped her tangled hair into a pony-tail. I was vaguely aware of the squeak and hiss of an old bike behind me. Then the noise stopped.

'Can I be next? I'll have a wash and blow dry, please.'

I spun round. A tall boy a couple of years older than me was perched on the bike. He held out a lock of his fair hair invitingly. Nicola giggled. I raised my eyebrows and sighed, but to my annoyance I could feel myself blushing.

He smiled at us. He wasn't really good looking, but he had a friendly sort of face.

16

'Are you both delivering papers? I'm standing in for Mark. You know Mark? A little kid with freckles. He lives next door to me. He can't do his round because he's gone camping with the school. That miserable old skinflint in there told him he'd lose the round if he took a few days off.'

'That miserable old skinflint happens to be our father,' I said coldly, and I marched off down the road, pulling Nicola with me.

Chapter 2

'There's a letter for you, Katherine,' Mum said when I got back from my newspaper round.

She was frying sausages. Nicola and I wanted tea and toast in the morning, but Dad was obsessed with the idea of everyone having a proper, cooked breakfast. Mum couldn't afford to give us bacon and eggs, which we wouldn't have minded. She went to a cheap butcher's shop in a back street and bought great, grey, gristly sausages.

'A letter?' I said, surprised. I hardly ever got any post. 'Only one sausage, Mum,'

The letter was waiting beside my plate, set neatly on the crumpled seersucker tablecloth. Miss Katherine Petworthy, 14a Waverton Parade, Kingtown. It was neat, educated writing on a plain, white envelope. The postmark was local.

'Open it then,' said Nicola, who was already munching stoically. The sausage still on her plate glistened with grease.

'Give me a chance. Why can't you *grill* them, Mum?'

'You want your toast, don't you? I can't put the sausages in the grill, not when I'm doing the toast.'

'You could keep the toast or the sausages warm in the oven, couldn't you?'

'And waste all that extra gas? Besides, your Dad likes his fry-up. He says they don't taste right, grilled.'

'They don't taste of anything but lard, fried. Can't you at least drain them properly?' I shuddered as Mum served up my fat, warty sausage, oozing grease from every pore.

'A bit of grease is good for you,' Mum said placidly.

'Who on earth can your letter be from? Why don't you open it?' said Nicola.

I ignored her. I'd recognised the handwriting. Oh God. The sausages became overwhelmingly important.

'I don't know what you mean, a bit of grease is good for you, I said to Mum, my tone becoming increasingly hectoring.

'Well, you know,' said Mum. 'Good. I should eat up your sausage, dear. Your Dad will be in for his breakfast any minute and you know it irritates him if you're finicky with your food.'

'Don't you know anything about current medical opinion? Grease is not good for you. It is very bad indeed. Didn't you know that eating too much fat and grease is one of the causes of coronory thrombosis?'

'Well, you're a bit young to worry about things like that. Do be a good girl and eat up your breakfast.'

'The sausage itself isn't good for me either. I presume you're under the mistaken belief that you're giving us protein.'

'It's meat. That's protein.'

'Where's the meat? I defy you to identify it amongst this muck,' I said, cutting my sausage in half and flamboyantly waving one end of it on my fork. 'It's not made of meat, Mum, it's made of breadcrumbs and cereal and gristle. That is not protein. If you have to buy sausages, why do you buy these awful ones?'

'They're very reasonable,' said Mum. 'Go on, stop being difficult and pop it in your mouth. Dad's coming.'

'If we've got to have a cheap cooked breakfast that contains lots of protein then why on earth don't you buy a simple tin of baked beans?' I continued.

Dad called impatiently from the stairs.

Mum hurriedly forked four sausages onto Dad's plate and fled downstairs to take his place in the shop.

Dad came into the kitchen and sat down.

'What's all this about baked beans? Horrible muck. Renders you not nice to be near, if you get my meaning. What are you hiding in your lap, Katherine?'

I'd snatched my letter off the table, but I hadn't been quick enough. I knew there was no way of hiding it now. I held it up so that Dad could see.

'Well, aren't you going to open it?'

'I suppose so.'

'You've gone all coy.' Dad suddenly choked on a sausage. 'Here, don't say it's a love letter!' he spluttered, as if it was the funniest joke in the world.

'It could be,' said Nicola, mistakenly thinking she was sticking up for me.

'Who'd get in a tizz over Miss Skinny Lizzy here?' Dad snorted.

'Lots of boys could,' said Nicola, ignoring my agonised expression. 'There was a boy chatting her up only this morning.'

'What? Which boy? Have you been seeing a boy, Katherine?' Dad had stopped joking.

'Nicola's just being silly,' I said quickly. 'It was just one of the newspaper boys.'

'Oh, them,' said Dad dismissively. 'Well, you tell them I'll be after them if they give you any lip. Cheeky little monkeys. Kids these days, act like they know it all. Had one the other day telling me he had a perfect right to a holiday any time he fancied. Can you credit it? I told him he could take his holiday, but he needn't bother coming back, not when I've got him down in the Holiday Book for the last two weeks of August. So what does he do? Only goes off on this bally camping business and sends some big friend in his place. I'd half a mind to send the friend off with a flea in his ear, but it's so damn difficult to get new boys nowadays so I had to go along with it. Open your letter then, Katherine.'

I eased the envelope open. I saw the embossed words Lady Margaret Lancaster High School for Girls at the top of the letter. I was right. My newly swallowed sausage stuck in my throat.

Dad's eyes were sharp.

'What's all this then?'

I pulled out the letter. It was very brief.

'I don't know,' I said hoarsely.

It was from Mrs Philpotts, my headmistress, asking me to come into school as soon as possible because she wanted to have a word with me.

'Well, what does she want you for?' said Dad, reading it upside-down.

'I don't know.'

'You must have some idea.'

Oh yes, I had a very good idea. She had probably glanced through some of our O level papers before parcelling them up to be sent to the examining board. She must have seen how terribly I'd done. Now she was going to . . . what? Scold me? Lecture me? Wrest my scholarship from me and tell me never to darken the doors of Lady Margaret Lancaster's again?

'I honestly don't have a clue,' I lied to Dad.

'It's this staying away from school except when you've got an exam. That's what it is. She's going to tick you off for playing truant. I knew you'd got hold of the wrong end of the stick.'

'Dad, I told you, you don't have to go into school if you haven't got an exam that day. It's not about that.'

'Then you'd better go and find out just what it is about, sharpish. Go and get into your uniform. I don't like the sound of this. You've never been in any trouble with the Head before.'

'She's not in any trouble now,' said Nicola. 'It could be about anything. She might be going to give Kath – Katherine an extra prize or something.'

'Oh dear me, how silly I am to jump to the wrong conclusion,' said Dad, with withering sarcasm. 'I should have asked for your advice in interpreting the letter, Nicola. Your perception and intellect are, of course, vastly superior to my own. And doubtless you are personally acquainted with Mrs Philpotts and more versed in her ways than I am. How many times have you met her? Well? Answer me!'

'You know I haven't ever met her,' Nicola mumbled, staring at her lap.

'Look at me when you talk to me! Why do you always have to adopt that awful, shifty pose? Sit up, girl, and straighten those shoulders. Now, just keep your nose out of it, all right? You don't know anything about Mrs Philpotts or her school. Do correct me if I'm wrong, but I believe you are the girl who tried two years running to get a place at Lady Margaret Lancaster's and failed both times?'

'Oh Dad, for goodness' sake! Don't be so hateful to her,' I shouted, crumpling my letter in my fist.

But I knew it would have been better to keep quiet. Dad told me to shut up and started lecturing Nicola properly. She fidgeted, struggled not to cry, and glanced worriedly at the clock. He knew he was making her late for school on top of everything else.

When at last he let her escape I gave her a quick hug in our bedroom. Her head drooped on my shoulder and she started sniffling.

'You can't start, Nic, you're late as it is, and if you go to school with red eyes then they'll tease you. Come on, let's get going,' I said, pushing her away. 'Pass us my skirt. Oh hell, I haven't got a clean white blouse, can I borrow one of yours? And I haven't got any tights. Does it look awful if I go without? My legs aren't too hairy, are they? I can't decide whether to start shaving them or not.'

I babbled on to try to distract both of us. When we went downstairs again Dad was still at the breakfast table sopping up sausage grease with a slice of bread, his digestion obviously not affected by the scene with Nicola. I whizzed her through the kitchen before he could start all over again.

We burst in on Mum in the shop and caught her in the middle of a Mars bar. She crammed the rest of it into her mouth, blushing furiously. She always insisted her weight problem was caused by some mysterious glandular trouble. She said she really didn't eat very much at all, and there was no point trying to go on a diet because she'd tried all that salad lark in the past and she hadn't lost a single pound. She refused to admit the fact that even when she was on the strict diet she ate at least six chocolate bars each day while she served in the shop.

I raised my eyebrows and sighed at Mum, as if I were her mother and she my giant, naughty child. Mum pretended not to notice and swallowed hurriedly.

'Mind how you go, girls,' she said, her teeth still coated in chocolate.

Nicola gave my hand a squeeze when we were outside the shop and then went running off to school, her short skirt flapping round her big, pink knees. I sighed, and set off in the opposite direction.

'Hey, I'm sorry I said that.'

I stared at the boy standing outside Berryman the Greengrocer. For a moment I didn't recognise him. Then I saw his bike propped against the wall. Mark's friend, the newspaper boy.

22

'I had no idea Mr Petworthy's your Dad,' he said.

He smiled at me timidly. He had brown eyes, although his hair was fair. It was nice hair, newly washed, rather fine, flopping forward over his forehead. I wondered how old he was. He was tall, at least five foot ten, and big. Not really fat. Just strong and stocky. But he wasn't a tough sort of boy at all. He was wearing fawn cords, rather baggy at the knees, and a blue and fawn checked shirt. They weren't stylish clothes and yet I quite liked them. They were comfortable clothes. He seemed comfortable too. I couldn't ever remember feeling comfortable with a boy before.

'Never mind. I suppose he *is* an old skinflint,' I said, and I smiled back at him.

'Are you off to school now?'

I'd forgotten I was dressed in my uniform. I nodded, feeling myself go hot. I prayed I wasn't blushing.

'I don't know that uniform. Where do you go?'

'Lady Margaret Lancaster's,' I mumbled.

'Oh. Very posh,' he said, but not nastily. 'I can see why your Dad has to count his pennies then.'

'Well – I've got a scholarship,' I said, and then knew I *must* be blushing.

'You m st be very brainy.'

'I – I didn't mean it to sound . . . I mean, I wasn't trying to show off,' I said.

'I know,' he said, getting his bike. 'Which way do you go? Do you get the bus? I'll walk you to the bus stop.'

So we set off together. I glanced round, just to make sure Dad wasn't peering out of our shop by some horrible chance. I couldn't believe I was actually walking down the road with a boy. People brushed past us, hurrying to work, obviously not finding it at all remarkable that Katherine Petworthy was walking along Waverton Parade with a boy.

I tried to think of something intelligent and interesting to say. I could think of nothing. I wondered how he came to be outside Berryman's. He must have finished Mark's round a good half-hour ago, no, longer than that. Surely he hadn't hung around all that time just to apologise to me?

'My name's Richard. What's yours?'

'Katherine.'

'What year are you in at school, Katherine?'

I hesitated. It was all Upper Fourths and Lower Fifths at Lady Margaret's.

'The fifth year.'

'So you're sixteen?'

'Well, no, I'm fifteen, actually. I'm younger than the others in my form. How old are you?'

'Seventeen.'

'Are you – are you at school?'

'No, I got fed up of it. I work at the *Comet* now.'

'The *Kingtown Comet*?' I began to feel really interested. 'Are you a reporter then?'

He laughed. 'No, I work in the print. My brother and my Dad do too. I've got an apprenticeship there.'

'I see.'

'What do you want to do when you leave school then, Katherine? I suppose you're staying on, doing A levels and going on to university and all that, seeing as you're brainy?'

'Well, I suppose so. If I've done all right in my O levels. I don't think I have.' I seemed to be telling everybody today.

'I'm glad I'm done with all that.'

'I got a letter from my headmistress this morning. That's why I'm going into school today. She wants to see me, and I'm scared it's because she knows I've mucked up my exams,' I said in a rush.

'Oh well. Exams aren't everything, are they?' said Richard, as if he really believed it. 'I hope you don't get into a row though.'

We were nearly at the bus stop.

'Do you – do you ever go out in the evenings?' Richard said, going red himself.

I shrugged awkwardly.

'Well, not really. I've always had homework and that.'

'Will you come out with me some time?' he said, not quite meeting my eyes.

I hesitated, wondering what on earth to say. I wasn't sure whether I wanted to or not. It was an enormous relief to find that there was at least one boy in the world who seemed to like me. But did I really like him? He wasn't at all like the dream men I'd made up. I'd always longed for someone poetic and

24

unusual and sensitive and creative and highly gifted.

'Go on, force yourself,' Richard joked, continuing to stare resolutely at my forehead.

'Well, I'd like to, but my father probably wouldn't let me. He's very old-fashioned. I think he'd be shocked at the idea of me going out with a boy,' I said truthfully.

'I'm not going to marry you or rape you or whatever,' said Richard. 'Couldn't we just go for a walk or go and have a hamburger or go to the pictures?' He suddenly looked at me properly. 'Unless you don't want to. I mean, I know I'm not exactly Superman . . .'

'Don't be silly,' I said. 'Look, I'll have to think about it.'

'There's a bus coming. You haven't got time to think about it. What about tonight? Shall I call for you at seven?'

'No! No, if I was going I'd have to meet you somewhere, but –'

'Okay, seven o'clock, at this bus-stop.'

'No, I can't, not tonight,' I gabbled, flustered, as the bus drew up.

'I'll be waiting here. Please come, Katy.'

No one had ever called me Katy before. It was a pretty, cute, pampered sort of name. I was much too plain and odd to be a Katy, but I liked being called it all the same.

'I'll try to come,' I said, smiling at him and getting on the bus.

He waved to me, grinning, and I waved back as the bus drove past him. I heard silly giggling, and turned round. There were two Lower Fourth girls sitting behind me, sniggering. I gave them a withering look and turned away again, but inside I went all shaky. I wondered what they thought of Richard.

Nearly all the girls in my own year had proper boy-friends but none of them were at all like Richard. They were mostly still at school for a start. Posh public schools. They had loud, plummy voices and they showed off a lot and played rugger and pretended to like real ale. I knew I couldn't bear a boy-friend like that. Anyway, what was I on about? Richard wasn't my boy-friend. We'd only just met. Perhaps he wasn't really serious about going out with me. Maybe he wouldn't turn up this evening. And I couldn't meet him, even if he did. Dad wouldn't let me.

There wouldn't be much point in going out with Richard anyway. I didn't have anything decent to wear. My jeans were so old and shabby now, and had started to show too much ankle. I'd die rather than go out in the new summer dress Mum had made for me. I thought of that awful, hideous dress and burned. I'd shown Mum the material I wanted in Rowbridge and Turner's. It was a subtle, smoky blue with a little white floral pattern, rather like a Laura Ashley design. It was cotton, practical and cheap. I'd pointed it out so carefully, and Mum had promised to buy that exact material as soon as she'd got enough money saved. I knew that my dress would still be pretty frightful. Mum was bad at dressmaking, even though she now used proper patterns instead of improvising from our Paper People fashion book. But I did comfort myself that at least it would be decent material this year.

But when Mum had finally scraped enough money out of the housekeeping she didn't go back to the department store where we'd seen the blue floral cotton. She went to the market instead, because it was cheaper, and she bought yards of some frightful, man-made, flimsy muck violently patterned with gigantic, peacock-blue roses. I burst into tears when I saw it.

'But it's almost the same as the first material and so much more reasonable,' Mum kept saying, utterly bewildered. 'It's blue, with flowers, just like the other one. Oh Katherine, don't cry like that, lovey. It's almost exactly the same.'

I said I'd sooner go round in my bra and school knickers than wear a dress in that terrible material, but I knew I'd have to. The market man wouldn't give Mum her money back, and there was no way she'd ever be able to afford to buy any of the blue cotton as well. The finished frock was worse than I'd imagined. Even Nicola had to bite her lip to stop herself laughing when I tried it on. If Richard saw me walking down Waverton Parade in those aggressive blue roses he'd run a mile in the opposite direction.

I was so taken up with worrying about my clothes and Richard and what on earth I was going to do at seven o'clock tonight that I forgot about the ominous letter tucked into my school skirt pocket. It wasn't until I got out at the bus stop nearest my school that my stomach clenched, and I remembered I had something far more worrying to cope with.

But Mrs Philpotts seemed pleased to see me when I put my head round her study door.

'Oh, it's you, Katherine! Come in, dear. Yes, I wanted to have a word with you.'

She gestured to the empty chair in front of her large desk.

'Take a pew.' She always used dated slang when she was trying to be matey.

I did as I was told. I was glad to sit down. My legs had started shaking. She didn't seem cross or disappointed. Her smile didn't waver. Her teeth were very white and even. I wondered if they might be false. I imagined Mrs Philpotts without teeth, as gummy as a baby.

'Well!' she said cheerfully, clasping her hands in front of her.

I didn't know whether to say anything in reply. I risked a very tentative smile myself.

'It's always a relief to get those old O levels over and done with, isn't it?' said Mrs Philpotts.

My throat dried. My smile died.

'Have a good long rest this summer, Katherine. I think you've deserved it, don't you? But first there's your Work Experience week.'

I nodded.

'Now, remind me. What career have you got in mind?' said Mrs Philpotts.

'Well, I'm not really sure. I want to go to university, of course – and then – maybe some sort of research?'

'Yes, that sounds very suitable. I'm sure you'll do splendidly. You're one of our brightest girls, Katherine.'

I wondered what she'd say when one of her brightest girls failed all eleven of her O levels.

'Now, as you know, we try to give you some kind of appropriate work experience, but it isn't always possible to fix each girl up with the exact sort of thing she had in mind. The hospital's always been very co-operative, and Barkley's Industries and J and C Mapletons are fine for those girls interested in Personnel Management and Secretarial work, but . . . anyway. As this isn't a university town it's a bit difficult, Katherine –'

'I understand, Mrs Philpotts, but it's all right. Miss Hyde says I can be in the class-room with her most of the time. She says I might even be able to teach some of the first years, just for half an hour or so.'

'Yes, I know Miss Hyde said you could. But I'm not so sure it's a very good idea.'

I stared at her, surprised.

'It's not what I really had in mind when I started this Work Experience scheme. I know I've always let some would-be teachers do their week at this school but I've always felt they're missing out on all the fun. The whole point is to try something new, something outside the cosy little world of Lady Margaret Lancaster's. Now this year there's just you and two other girls who want some kind of teaching experience, so I've been able to fix you up with a special treat. The headmistress of Lingfield Road Nursery School happens to be a great friend of mine, and she says she'd be happy to have you doing your work experience at her little school next week.'

Chapter 3

I trailed miserably round the town for a while because I couldn't face the thought of going home. Dad would want to know every single word Mrs Philpotts had said. He'd be relieved but irritated to find out she had simply wanted to see me to tell me I was being sent to the nursery school next week. He'd think it a daft waste of time. I could just hear him going on about cheap labour and wondering how playing with a load of whiny toddlers was going to help me become a professor.

Mum would probably feel pleased for me. She loved all very small children and assumed that everyone else did too. They were the only people with whom she could be completely at ease. When they got old enough to go to school they got old enough to snigger at her size, but at two or three they accepted – even admired – her great bulk. They were always creeping round the counter, climbing up her vast peaks and nestling in her valleys. Mum enveloped them in her massive arms, genuinely not minding if they wiped their snotty noses against her cheek or smeared their sticky fingers on her frock. She listened to them patiently as they stuttered out banal little sentences, encouraged even the shyest to lisp its way through a nursery rhyme or advertising jingle, and popped a chocolate drop into every drooling little mouth.

She was worse with babies. She loved them all indiscriminately, even the hideous or handicapped. She begged for a cuddle with the scabby and the smelly. They were too little for party pieces, so Mum performed on their behalf. 'Who's a little poppet then, eh? Have you got a smile for me then, a smile for Auntie? Yes you have. Come on then. Lickle smile?' She'd burble baby talk and blow baby bubbles, a great, grisly parody of a baby herself.

At least Nicola would be sympathetic because she knew I

hated children. She said she hated them too, and we had even once played a game in which we aimed an invisible machine-gun at the most sickening sweetie-pies, imagining their pretty little faces exploding like shaken cans of coke – but I knew her heart wasn't in it. I'd caught her squatting down having cosy chats with winsome tots. When she grew up she'd probably succumb utterly, just like Mum.

She wouldn't really understand my horror at the thought of spending a week at Lingfield Road Nursery School. I'd tried explaining to Mrs Philpotts, but it was hopeless. She'd made up her mind that she had organised a great treat for me, and she was determined that I should feel thrilled. She prided herself on her modern feminist ideas, but she was reactionary enough to think that all girls liked small children.

Small children didn't think much of me either. Babies cried when I went near them. Toddlers kicked out at me with their silly square feet. Their older brothers and sisters waggled their tongues at me and called me names. They were all the same. They sensed something about me. Just one look and they knew I was queer, odd, different, the one to pick on and pester. I thought of a whole week coping with a roomful of intractable infants and I actually groaned out loud, so that an assistant in Rowbridge and Turner nudged her friend and they both giggled.

I had gone into the shop to have another look at the subtle blue material. It looked even prettier this time. *Why* couldn't my stupid mother have bought it? I went to look at the clothes in Star Shop, Rowbridge and Turner's idea of a boutique. I fingered several outfits wistfully. They were all a bit garish and thrown together, I could see that, but they all looked *right*. I wandered round and round each circular clothes rack, as if performing a complicated dance, trying to make up my mind what I'd choose if my school purse contained twenty-five pounds instead of twenty-five pence. I wasn't that keen on the colours, either gaudy primaries or insipid pastels, but what about the white broderie anglaise blouse or the black trousers cut in the latest style?

I saw myself in them, grown-up, flamboyant, poised, sexy . . . but when I took them into the changing room I came sadly down to earth. It was dreadfully embarrassing for a start because there were two other girls in there, calmly stripping off right down to their neat little Marks and Sparks bikini pants. One wasn't wearing a bra. She had lovely breasts, firm and white with nipples like pink Smarties.

I didn't really mind exposing my own childish chest, but I was terrified that they'd see my knickers. I only had ghastly great grey school knickers or some ancient, floppy, white ones with baggy legs that I seemed to have been wearing most of my life. I was wearing the white ones today – only they weren't even white any longer, more a depressing dishcloth beige, although they were honestly clean on that morning.

I pulled the trousers up before I took my skirt off, fumbling with unseen zips and buttons and elastic. After all that struggle I looked awful in the blouse and trousers. They were too big for me for a start although they were the smallest size. The blouse hung down foolishly at the front, exposing a great deal of my collar-bone and inadequate flesh. The trousers sagged unattractively because I lacked decent hips and a provocative bottom. I wanted to burst into tears as I looked at myself in the mirror and saw dozens of equally frightful reflections of myself all around the changing room.

The two girls with pretty breasts and decent underwear charitably averted their eyes. I hurriedly changed back into my school uniform. It was dowdy and hideous, but at least it fitted. But I still looked dreadful all the same. How could I have come out without tights? I looked at my skinny, white legs in horror. And my hair! I'd messed it up scrambling in and out of blouses and I didn't have a brush with me. It stood up wildly, an unkempt black frizz exploding in every direction.

Why on earth did Richard want to go out with me? Perhaps he was just kidding me. He couldn't really like me. Of course he wouldn't turn up tonight. Maybe it was his sick way of getting his own back on Dad because he'd been nasty to his friend? Anyway, I'd probably only make a fool of myself even if he did really want me to go out with him. And it would involve so many lies to Dad. I just didn't have the nerve.

So there was no point fussing about clothes, not if I wasn't going out anyway. I'd stay at home wearing my old jeans and play Paper People with Nicola.

I returned the boutique clothes to the right rack and went

back to the dressmaking department. Nicola and I had been using the same fashion book for ages. We'd cut out nearly all the best people. I would buy us a new fashion book. Nicola would be thrilled. But when I asked the girl behind the counter she said that old Style and Simplicity and McCalls now cost a pound a copy and the Vogue ones were even dearer. It would take ages to save up. It would be more sensible to draw my own people, even if the ones I invented often worried Nicola.

I went down to the art department to buy myself a new drawing book, but they were far too expensive too, even the big fuzzy pads for little kids. I sighed irritably. There didn't seem anything in the whole stupid store that cost twenty five pence or less. It was a completely useless amount of money. I couldn't be bothered to save it up carefully. I decided to go and waste it on a coffee and to hell with it.

I got the lift up to the posh coffee shop on the third floor. On Nicola's birthday Mum had once treated us to doughnuts and orange squash in Rowbridge and Turner, but that had only been in the cafeteria downstairs. Nicola and I had always longed to go to the coffee shop. It was light and airy and elegant, with pine furniture and cobalt blue tablecloths and white china with little blue dots. There was a counter running the length of the shop, an incredible mosaic of beautiful luxury food: open sandwiches, bowls of salad, croissants, huge cream cakes, Danish pastries, all glistening like precious jewels.

I knew I couldn't afford anything but a coffee but I deliberated for a long time in the queue pretending I was rich enough to choose whatever I fancied. I couldn't decide whether I'd have the prawn sandwich garnished with egg and lettuce and little seedless grapes or a wedge of Black Forest gateau with six scarlet cherries nestling in the cream topping. A big, tall girl like Nicola was standing in front of the cakes, looking as if she was learning them by heart.

I moved up in the queue and looked at the girl properly. It *was* Nicola.

I stared at her, astonished. It was five to eleven. She was supposed to be finishing an energetic double Games lesson at Malford Road Comprehensive.

'Nicola!'

She spun round, her hand flying to her mouth, her elbows

jerking out so wildly she nearly knocked a plate of strawberry tarts flying.

'Hey, Nic, watch out!'

She had gone very white and looked as if she might be about to cry.

'Have you got any money?'

She shook her head, but then found five pence and a few pennies in her pocket.

'We'll share a coffee, eh? And we'll get a little packet of biscuits. You choose. Go on, have Bourbon, you know you like those the best.'

I got her sitting down at a table in the corner. I'd taken extra sugar and offered a lump to her on the palm of my hand.

'Here you are, Dobbin.'

'Neigh,' said Nicola faintly, picking up the sugar lump and eating it. 'How did you get on with Mrs Philpotts?'

'Oh, it was just about my Work Experience. Never mind about that now. What about you?'

'What about me?'

'Oh Nic! What are you *doing* here?'

Nicola chewed unnecessarily at her sugar lump and didn't answer.

'Didn't you feel well at school?'

Nicola nodded uncertainly.

'Mmm. Yes, I – I felt sick. So I asked if I could come home.'

'Liar! You felt *sick*? You were licking your lips over those cakes just now. Did you even go to school today?'

'Yes,' said Nicola. 'Of course I did.'

'You didn't. You can't have. Oh Nic, you can tell me, can't you?'

'You won't tell Mum and Dad?'

'Don't be daft.' I was feeling hurt. I'd thought Nicola and I were so close. Nicola always seemed to think the world of me. I'd thought she told me absolutely everything.

'All right then, I didn't go. I haven't been going much all this term,' said Nicola, nibbling at a Bourbon.

I was amazed. I'd thought she'd just played truant today, probably because Dad had got on at her and she was feeling upset. That seemed astonishing enough. I simply couldn't

33

take it in that she'd been staying off school regularly. Nicola, who was frightened of the dark, who burst into tears at the slightest thing. I was the one who was supposed to have all the spark, and yet I'd never once dared stay away from school, even though I'd often dreaded going.

'You won't tell, will you?' Nicola said anxiously, finishing her biscuit and helping herself to another.

'I just can't believe it. I never dreamt . . . Why didn't you tell me before?'

'I didn't dare.'

'But all those times when I asked you what sort of a day you had and you rabbited on about French and rounders and school mince and Jennifer Johnson's new boy-friend – were you making it all up?'

'Sh!' Nicola flapped her hand in the air to get me to lower my voice. 'Yes, most of it. I did go for a bit, just after Easter – but then it got so awful, and they were being so horrible to me –'

'Who?'

'Oh, Pam and Maureen Henderson and all that lot. They said things and I tried not to take any notice but I always ended up crying and that made them even worse. And then they started scribbling all over my books and stealing things out of my school-bag . . .' Nicola was nearly in tears talking about it, her face very red.

'Here.' I passed the coffee over to her. 'You said they were nicer this year, that they were getting quite friendly.'

'I know I did. But I was just making it up. It got so awful. Lessons weren't too bad, but it started to be every Break, and they followed me everywhere. I didn't know what to do. One of the other girls said I ought to go to Mr Symons and tell him, but can you imagine what they'd be like after I'd done that? So I just stopped going to school.'

'But what on earth have you been doing with yourself?'

'Oh, nothing much. I walk about. Sometimes I go to the library, or I look round the shops, or I might go down by the river. If it's warm I sunbathe for a bit.'

'Hasn't anyone ever come up to you and asked you why you're not at school?'

'No. Well, this man did once, down by the river, but he was just being friendly. Nobody's ever said anything nasty. Lots of

34

children bunk off from school nowadays.'

'And the school hasn't even done anything, even though you've been absent all this time! It just shows what a lousy place it is.'

'Well, they wrote a letter.'

'What letter?'

'To Mum and Dad. There was this letter, it came just as I got back from doing my newspaper round, I saw it on the mat. There was my school crest on the envelope, so I whipped it up and waited and then opened it in the lav. It was from Mr Symons asking if I was ill, and saying that he was getting concerned about me, and he'd be grateful if Mum or Dad could go to the school to see him.'

'So what did you do?'

'I tore it up, of course. He hasn't written again. Here, you know your letter this morning? I thought just for a minute you might have – but of course *you'd* never do something like staying off school.' Nicola sounded bitter.

'I don't like school either, you know I don't. And I get teased too.'

'Yes, but your girls aren't really hateful, not the way mine are. And anyway, you're so clever and always top of everything. I can't even be good at lessons.'

'You're in the top stream.'

'Big deal. I'm not top though, am I? I'm not even in the top three, and Dad says Malford's just a glorified Secondary Modern and all the kids there are practically educationally subnormal –'

'He just talks a lot of rubbish, you know he does. Here, leave me *one* biscuit, greedy-guts. And pass the coffee. I still can't see why you couldn't tell me. I thought we were supposed to be best friends as well as sisters?'

'We are,' said Nicola fiercely, bending her head. 'But I couldn't tell you, Kath. I didn't want you to look down on me.' A tear splashed onto her arm.

'Oh Nic,' I said, reaching out and holding her wrist.

I didn't look down on her at all. In fact, although I knew it was stupid and self-defeating to play truant from school, I couldn't help admiring Nicola.

'Anyway, it'll be the summer holidays soon. Then you won't

have to pretend any more. But you'll have to start going again in the Autumn.'

'No,' said Nicola. 'I'm not going back there. Never.

'Don't be silly. You've got to have some sort of education.'

'Why?'

'If you have to ask why, then it's obvious you need to be educated,' I said briskly.

'No, but I don't see why I need to know much more. I can read anything I need to know in books. I don't want to go on to university or anything like you, so I don't need to pass any exams.'

'I've never heard such nonsense in all my life. What are you going to do with yourself then? What sort of career are you going to have?'

'By the time I get to be grown-up it won't be possible to have a career, not the sort you mean. It's bad enough now, all the redundancies and the recession and everything.'

I was surprised. Nicola usually knew so little about current affairs, but now she sounded properly informed.

'You're going to need qualifications all the more then, if we're all going to be fighting for jobs.'

'There aren't going to be all these jobs. You'll probably be all right, all the really brainy people. But not average people like me.'

'Who have you been talking to?'

'No one,' said Nicola hurriedly. 'I might be thick but I'm not that thick, you know. I can work some things out for myself. Can I finish the coffee?'

'Yes, okay. So what are you going to do? Nothing at all?'

'I'll go on the dole. I'll be poor, but I'm used to that. I'll just loaf about like I'm doing now. It's all right. It's better than school and it's probably better than work.'

She didn't sound like Nicola at all. It made me uncomfortable and bewildered. I was so used to telling Nicola what to do. She was usually as soft and compliant as Sniffle, Woffle and Muffle. Learning that Nicola had been practising this daring deception for months was as astonishing as if I'd learnt that our toy animals led an independent life of their own. I needed to slap her back down to size.

36

'You are a fool. The school will keep writing, and sooner or later they'll send a truant officer round to see Dad,' I said nastily.

'They don't bother nowadays,' said Nicola, but she didn't sound very certain. She drained the coffee.

'What are you going to do now? You'd better come home with me. Pretend you weren't well at school.'

'No. No, you go back. I'll stay out.'

'But you can't. It must get so boring just hanging about.'

'I'm used to it.'

'Well look, I'll come round the shops with you for a bit.'

'It's okay. I'll be all right.'

'I want to.'

'Then I'd love you to, you know I would,' said Nicola, snuggling into me, suddenly her old silly self again. 'Kath – you're not cross with me, are you?'

'No, of course I'm not.'

'Shall we go and look at the toy department?'

I sighed, but we went there all the same, and I even played a game with Nicola where we were both terribly rich little girls of three and five and our parents had told us we could choose three toys each, and it didn't matter how much they cost. Nicola chose the biggest doll, the biggest teddy bear and a very yucky 'just like Mother' set of toy housework implements. I wanted to be very feminist, but I really didn't fancy a toy train or car at all, so I chose a huge bag of wooden building bricks, a paintbox and a rocking-horse.

Nicola dragged me off to the furniture department next, to choose the furniture for our imaginary nursery, but the little tables and chairs and cots reminded me of next week. I told Nicola that I was going to have to go to the nursery school.

'Maybe I'll play truant too. I can't stand the idea.'

'I think it'd be lovely,' said Nicola.

'There, I knew you were really as bad as Mum. Hey, that's something you could do. Be a nursery teacher. You'd be good at it. So get yourself back to school and get some O levels and then . . . ' But my voice tailed away. I thought of my own O levels. What was I doing lecturing my sister when I'd probably end up without any O levels myself? The familiar churning started in my stomach. Goose-pimples puckered my arms and I shivered.

I wondered about telling Nicola that I was sure I'd failed them. But she wouldn't believe me. I'd have to explain to convince her, go into details about the awful dreamlike unreality of each examination, tell her about the three week nightmare of inadequacy and incompetence . . . but I couldn't bear to relive it all.

It had been so simple telling Richard.

'Here, Nic, you know that boy this morning – '

'What boy?' said Nicola vaguely, sinking into a huge leather armchair. 'Feel this, Kath, it's like sitting on a cloud. Let's choose furniture for our flat for when we're grown-up. This chair's mine for a start.'

'You'll have an assistant over in a minute. Come on, get up. You know, Mark's older friend, the boy who did his round for him.'

'Oh, him. What about him then?'

I hesitated, feeling absurdly shy. Wait till Nicola knew he'd hung around waiting for me all that time and had actually asked me out!

'I think he fancied you,' said Nicola, before I could say anything. 'Pity he wasn't really interesting, eh?'

'What do you mean?'

'Well. You know,' said Nicola, 'I mean, you wouldn't want to go out with him, would you?'

'Why?' I said sharply.

'Well, he's . . .' Nicola wrinkled her nose.

'Do stop sprawling in that chair. And stop pulling stupid faces. No wonder it irritates Dad. Come *on*,' I said, and I marched off quickly so that Nicola had to run to catch me up.

Chapter 4

I decided that I certainly wasn't going to go out with Richard now. But at six o'clock I started to get very fidgety. The evening loomed, long and flat and depressing. We'd already eaten and washed up. Dad demanded high tea on the dot of half-past five when he shut up the shop. Most of the shops on the Waverton Parade stayed open until half-past six now. The sweet-shop at the other end stayed open until half-past seven every single evening. Business might well have picked up if Dad had been prepared to be more competitive with his opening hours, but the thought enraged him.

'I'm not keeping Paki hours and that's that! Whose bally country is it? We've always shut at half-past five and we always will. That's when I like my grub and that's when I'm going to eat it.'

After his tea Dad settled in his armchair with the *Daily Express* and dozed and grumbled his way through the evening. He had cocoa and a ginger biscuit whilst watching the nine o'clock news, and was usually on his way up to bed by the weather forecast. Mum sat on the sofa (she was too large to fit comfortably into the other armchair) and carefully read counter copies of *Woman* and *Woman's Own* and *Woman's Realm* and *Woman's Weekly*, keeping one eye on the television. Dad liked to select the programmes for the evening, even though he slept seventy-five per cent of the time. Most of the programmes Mum liked Dad called drivel, and if she tried to switch over while he was asleep he nearly always woke with a suspicious snort and caught her with her hand on the dial.

I didn't want to spend my evening in the living-room with them. I didn't want to spend it in the bedroom either, playing Paper People with Nicola. But I didn't want to spend the evening with Richard, did I?

By half-past six I was starting to panic. He wasn't really the sort of boy to play a joke on me. He would probably be there at the bus stop at seven, waiting for me. It was going to be horrible for him standing there, the minutes ticking by. It wouldn't be so bad if I never had to see him again, but he'd be coming tomorrow morning to do Mark's paper round. What on earth was I going to do then? I'd feel so awful. He might be really angry with me. Suppose he stood at the bus-stop for ages, wasting half his evening? Oh God, suppose he *didn't* wait patiently? He knew where I lived. Suppose he came round to the shop to see what was keeping me?

I couldn't risk it. I had to go to the bus-stop and see Richard. I needn't go out with him. I could just tell him that my Dad wouldn't let me, and then rush straight back home.

I was still in my school uniform, with my hair sticking out in a wild bush and an unpleasant taste of kipper in my mouth from tea. I flew to the bathroom in a panic. I mightn't be going out with him, I mightn't even think much of him, but I didn't want him to see me all dowdy and tangly and kippery.

I washed and cleaned my teeth thoroughly, and then stood in the bedroom in my horrible baggy knickers wondering what on earth to wear. *Not* the monstrous blue dress. Jeans. And tennis shoes. But which top? My T-shirt emphasised my flat chest. I fumbled through my own clothes and then Nicola's without success. Then I found a length of tartan hair ribbon belonging to Nicola and had an inspiration. I pulled my school blouse back on and arranged the ribbon like a tie. It didn't look too bad.

I attacked my hair with a brush, dragging it back into a pony-tail of sorts, although little springy fronds escaped whenever I moved my head. My face looked very pale and plain with my hair scraped back. I didn't have any make-up but I got my old paintbox and rubbed a little vermilion into my cheeks and tried some burnt sienna on my eyelids.

'What on earth are you doing?' said Nicola, coming up to our bedroom and staring at me.

'Never you mind,' I said sharply. I hadn't forgiven her for unintentionally insulting Richard.

'That's my hair ribbon,' she said, getting on her bed and feeling for Sniffle, Woffle and Muffle.

40

'You don't mind if I borrow it, do you? Of course, if Madam objects then I'll take it off immediately,' I snapped, one eye on my Magic Roundabout alarm. Nearly ten to seven. Oh God.

'Of course I don't mind,' said Nicola unhappily, locating the last animal and burying her nose in Muffle. 'Why are you being so nasty to me, Kath?'

'I'm not being nasty,' I lied, staring in the mirror sideways. I still looked so flat. If only Nicola would get out of the bedroom I could try stuffing a couple of hankies in my bra and see if that looked any better.

'Are you going out, Kath?'

I grunted, scrubbing at my cheeks. I'd been a little heavy-handed with the vermilion.

'Where are you going?' said Nicola, valiantly not reminding me that I'd promised to play Paper People with her.

'Out.'

She looked at me mournfully with her big Bambi eyes but I wouldn't give in and tell her. She'd been so dismissive about Richard. What a cheek she had! We weren't so special ourselves. And as a matter of fact Nicola was even less prepossessing than I was. She was tall and awkward and overweight and she didn't wash her hair often enough. What right did she have to criticise Richard? Anyway, why should I tell her absolutely everything? She had been playing truant for months and yet she'd never breathed a word about it to me.

Dougal's tail wagged relentlessly as time ticked on. Why on earth was I so nervous? I wasn't even going out with Richard. All I had to do was tell him I couldn't make it. Thirty seconds of conversation. Unless – *should* I go? I didn't really want to, but at least I'd be able to boast truthfully at school that I'd actually been out with a boy. And it sounded so wet, bleating that Dad wouldn't let me. He'd think me pathetic. It would probably be much easier going out with him for an hour or two.

I'd only just been to the lav but I had to rush to go again, and then I went down to face Dad, Nicola trailing behind me.

'I – I'm just going out,' I said.

'What do you mean, you're just going out?' Dad repeated predictably.

I knew there was only one sort of lie that he would accept.

41

'I'm going over to Miss Hyde's – you know, my English teacher. I bumped into her at school this morning and she asked me round to her place this evening. She wants to suggest some holiday reading.'

'Why on earth didn't you say so before?'

'Well, I didn't really want to go. I wondered about trying to get out of it,' I said. 'You know I don't really like going round to her flat.'

I'd been to Miss Hyde's twice before. We had both been nervous and self-conscious, and there had been long gaps in between our conversation.

'I don't know what you're on about. I think it's a great compliment, your teacher wanting to see you to give you that extra bit of encouragement. It's obvious this Miss Hyde realises you're pretty exceptional.'

'I wish you wouldn't talk like that, Dad.'

'There's no point in false modesty, is there? Look, the silly girl's blushing! No, wait a minute. Come over here. What have you got on your cheeks?'

'Nothing! Oh Dad, I'm going to be late, I must go.'

'You ought to wear a frock if you're going out visiting,' Mum said. 'Especially as it's a teacher.'

'That's right, you're not going out in those awful jeans, girl,' said Dad. 'We don't want Miss Hyde to think you don't know any better. We might be poor but we don't have gutter standards. You look like any scruffy yob off the street in those jeans.'

'For Heaven's sake, Miss Hyde will probably be wearing jeans herself,' I said hurriedly. 'She told me to wear something old, because she wants me to look in her attic for all these dusty old books. I must go now. 'Bye.'

I rushed out of the house before Dad remembered Miss Hyde lived in a basement flat and didn't have an attic. I needed to go to the lav *again* but I didn't dare go back. I heard St Agatha's church clock striking seven so I hurried up Waverton Parade.

There were several people waiting at the bus-stop but I was too far away to see if any of them were Richard. I kept on walking although my skeleton seemed to have disintegrated and my floppy, boneless legs could hardly support me. My arms refused to co-ordinate with my legs. My head sagged as I suddenly recognised Richard.

He'd changed out of his comfortable check shirt and cords. He was wearing an ostentatious cream jacket, dark brown trousers and a white shirt. The cheap jacket didn't fit him very well, especially at the shoulders. Even his hair was spoilt, slicked back and painfully neat. Oh God, what on earth was I doing? I could be cosily playing Paper People with Nicola instead of approaching this badly dressed, frightening stranger.

But it was too late to turn and run home. Richard's arm suddenly shot up and he waved awkwardly. I waved too, feeling an utter fool. I carried on walking. We both smiled stiffly, teeth clenched. As I got nearer my smile became more and more strained. I had to look away, pretending to be searching for something in my pocket. I found my hankie and blew my nose just for something to do. My hands were shaking.

'Hello Katy,' said Richard.

I wasn't so sure I liked the nickname now. It sounded a bit pretentious and silly.

'Hello Richard.' My voice didn't sound like mine at all. It was all squeaky and affected.

'I hope you haven't got a cold,' said Richard.

'What? Oh no,' I said, stuffing my handkerchief back in my pocket. My nose felt wet and I wondered with horror if I'd somehow smeared mucus all over it. I tried brushing it casually with the back of my hand. Nothing came away but I remained uneasy.

'I didn't think you'd come,' said Richard.

'Oh. Well. I can't really stay out long.'

'So where would you like to go?'

I stared at him, wondering what on earth to reply. What a stupid question! Why couldn't he just take me somewhere, for goodness' sake? Where *did* people go on dates?

'I don't mind. We'll go wherever you like,' I said.

'No, you say. It's up to you,' Richard insisted.

The people waiting at the bus-stop were obviously listening to our less than sparkling conversation. They would start smirking soon.

43

'Shall we just walk for a bit?' I said desperately.

Richard looked surprised, but nodded. At least it meant we left the bus queue behind us. We walked along briskly, keeping a careful foot or more between us. Richard glanced at me every so often. Sometimes he smiled and I smiled back uncomfortably. Once he gave me a silly wink and I felt foolish. I couldn't think of a single thing to say. Why on earth had I thought him so easy to talk to? But he didn't look like himself any more. The jacket made him look older, flashy, frightening. And his hair looked so awful slicked back like that. It looked as if he'd put grease on it. He was whistling under his breath. Perhaps he was bored. *I* was bored. What was the point of this?

We were nearing the Ploughman's Arms on the corner of Waverton Parade.

'Would you like a drink?' said Richard.

I hesitated. At least it would be something to do. I'd never been in a pub in my life. Dad said spirits destroyed your liver, beer rotted the gut, and public houses were dens of iniquity. I was quite curious to see what one of these dens was like. But weren't you supposed to be eighteen? I looked even younger than I really was. How awful if I got turned out the minute I crossed the pub threshold!

'Not really.'

'Okay.'

He started whistling again. We turned the corner of the Parade and started walking up Brook Street. A gust of wind blew, ruffling his carefully arranged hair. He quickly ran his fingers through it and then caught me looking at him. His smile was sheepish.

'Have you put haircream on it?' I asked.

'No. It's water. My Mum attacked it with a wet comb just as I was coming out. It looks daft, doesn't it?'

'No,' I said. 'Well – a bit.'

'It'll dry soon. I hope. Honestly, mothers! Is your Mum like that?'

'Not really. But my father makes up for her. He's always on at me.'

'But he let you come out with me tonight.'

'Well, not exactly.'

'What do you mean?'

'He thinks I'm having supper with one of my teachers.'

'Oh.' Richard sounded a bit put out. There was a sudden constraint between us, just when it looked as if things might turn out all right.

I tried to think of something else to say. I rehearsed all sorts of things inside my head, but they all sounded so stupid I kept quiet. We walked the whole length of Brook Street in silence and started on Petersfield Avenue. The Magpie pub half-way down the street was blaring out pop music. The door was open at the side, and I could see weird white and purple flashing lights.

'I wonder what's going on in there? See those lights?' I said.

'It's a disco,' said Richard, staring at me as if I was mad.

I felt idiotic. Of course it must be a disco.

'Haven't you ever been to a disco?' he said.

'Oh yes,' I lied quickly.

Richard didn't look convinced.

'Would you like to go to this one?'

I thought he would, so I said yes, although I wasn't at all sure it was a good idea. I was right.

The disco was held in a very small, airless room. At first there were only a few people there, but about eight o'clock a whole crowd started pouring in, and by half-past it was so packed we could barely move. The music was so startlingly loud that I wanted to cower away from it. I couldn't hear a word Richard was saying, even when he shouted right into my ear. I couldn't see him properly either. The white and purple lights flashed continuously until the whole room seemed to be spinning. I could scarcely make sense of the shapes of people and tables and chairs and drinks; they were just a meaningless kaleidoscope of pattern. The only sense left unaffected was my sense of smell. The room reeked of beer and scent and sweat. It was such a pervasive smell that it seemed part of me too, and I bent my head and sniffed anxiously, terrified that I might be contributing to the atmosphere. My school blouse stuck to my back even before Richard and I tried to dance.

I had practised dancing with Nicola. She was so hopelessly uncoordinated that I seemed rhythmic and graceful by comparison. But at the disco I couldn't seem to move to the right beat and my arms and legs and head wouldn't work in unison.

45

It was both a relief and an embarrassment to see that Richard wasn't any better at dancing either. He moved too enthusiastically, waving his arms around and taking big steps. He was obviously also feeling the heat. Beads of sweat shone eerily on his brow so that he looked luminous in the odd light.

I was afraid people were staring at us, although when I looked round nobody seemed aware of our existence. I thought I saw people I knew, customers from the shop, but everyone looked so different in the flashing lights that I couldn't be sure. Even I seemed different. My white school blouse became an incredible shade of violet in the light and I admired the strange new shade as I jerked my arms in approximate time to the music. Luckily lots of other girls were wearing jeans too, but I could see the tennis shoes were a big mistake. I needed spiky high heels. They'd have been a help to my height too. There was a great discrepancy between my five foot and Richard's nearly six foot. I was bobbing around his chest all the time.

When they put on a slow record most of the couples danced cheek to cheek. That was impossible for Richard and me, but he didn't even try to dance closely. He held me stiffly, almost at arm's length. His hand was as hot and wet as mine.

We weren't very good at dancing together. I couldn't seem to anticipate which way he was going to go and we kept clashing awkwardly.

'I'm scared I'm going to trample you to death,' he yelled in my ear. 'Let's have a drink. What would you like?'

I wasn't at all sure what to ask for. I didn't know if they sold things like coke or lemonade in pubs. I wasn't familiar with the names of many alcoholic drinks. I wasn't fool enough to ask for beer or whisky or gin and I couldn't think of anything else.

'What about a fruit juice?' Richard suggested.

I nodded, relieved. He left me in a corner for a very long time when he got the drinks. Boys kept pushing past me, often rudely looking me up and down. I grew even hotter. I was terrified that one of them might start chatting me up but none of them seemed remotely interested. I wasn't sure whether I was relieved or disappointed. After a while I peered round anxiously but I couldn't see any sign of Richard. It suddenly struck me that he might have got so fed up with me that he'd walked out on me. I started to feel sick but then I felt someone tapping my shoulder and it was Richard, carrying two half-full glasses.

'Sorry! You can't move in the bar – and some fool barged into me just as I got served.'

'Oh dear. Look, you've got some on your jacket.'

'Where?' Richard peered gloomily at the large stain. 'Oh hell. Mick'll murder me.'

'Who's Mick?'

'My brother. He lent me the jacket as a special favour. I didn't really have anything suitable to wear. Most of my clothes, well – they're either too casual or else they're too formal, if you see what I mean,' Richard mumbled, obviously embarrassed.

'I haven't got the right clothes either,' I said. I looked down at myself. 'As you can see.'

'I think you look great,' said Richard, as if he really meant it. 'I love that blouse and tie. It really suits you.'

'It's only my old school blouse and my sister's hair ribbon. I put them on in desperation. My parents had a moan at me because they don't like me wearing jeans much but I didn't take any notice.'

'My Mum can't stick jeans either. You'll never guess what she said I ought to wear tonight. My best suit. I got it for my cousin's wedding. It's a hideous suit for a start, and I look a right berk in it, especially now it's got a bit small for me. You wouldn't have gone out with me, not if I'd turned up wearing that.'

'Well, you should just see the dress my mother wanted me to wear!' I said, and I told Richard all about the hideous blue frock. I'd never dreamt I'd ever tell anyone and turn it all into a joke. But somehow I'd got comfortable with Richard again and I didn't mind him knowing and laughing. We were talking so easily now although it was a strain shouting to make ourselves heard.

'I'm getting hoarse. Shall we go somewhere where we can talk properly?' Richard said.

'Yes, let's.'

We stood up to go, trying to thread our way through the mass of people.

'I'd better go first. Here, hold tight,' said Richard, taking hold of my hand. 'I don't want to lose you.'

I held on to him and he led me safely to the door. It seemed astonishingly dark and still and silent outside. Richard kept hold of my hand but his arm was a little stiff. Our hands were very damp. I hoped it wasn't just from me.

'That's better. Now we can talk,' said Richard.

There was an inevitable silence.

'Are you frantically trying to think of something to say?' I said.

'Yes. Are you?'

'Yes.'

We laughed shakily.

'You didn't really like the disco, did you?' said Richard.

'Yes I did.'

'It's all right. I don't like them much either. Where would you like to go now? Are you hungry?'

'I really ought to be going home soon.'

'But it's not even nine o'clock yet!'

'Yes, but my father will be expecting me back soon. Honestly Richard. He's so strict. You don't know what he's like.'

'Why didn't you tell him about me?' Richard said. 'Is it – are you ashamed of me or something?'

'Don't be silly,' I said quickly. 'No, of course I'm not. It's not you. It's any boy. My father is so old-fashioned it's just not true. He's really Victorian.'

'You're not going to get yourself into trouble with him, are you?' said Richard. 'That's the last thing I'd want. I mean, if your Dad found out – well, he wouldn't hit you or anything, would he?'

'Oh, he doesn't ever hit me. He's not that sort of strict. No, he just gets in a state and shouts and says horrible things. I suppose that doesn't sound that bad, but it is when he's going on at me.'

'And what time is he expecting you back?'

'About half-past nine, I suppose. He goes to bed then, believe it or not.'

'Well, if I promise to get you back home by then will you come and have a quick snack first?'

He took me to a café called 'Albert's' just round the corner.

48

Nicola and I had noticed it when it opened about a year ago and had admired it wistfully. I liked the Victorian décor, all chocolate brown paint and busts of Albert and potted palms in brass pots. Nicola liked the menu, and had spent hours wondering whether she'd prefer the Knickerbocker Glory or the Maple Walnut Ice-cream Waffles.

'What would you like?' Richard asked, when we were sitting down.

I looked at the prices worriedly.

'Just a coffee would be lovely.'

'Come on, you must have more than that. I'm going to have a hamburger. You have one too. You look as if you need a square meal.' He picked up my skinny wrist. 'Look at this nobbly bit! There's nothing of you.' He put his own large hand round my wrist. His hand wasn't damp any more, just pleasantly warm. His fingers were square and strong, with short, clean fingernails. I liked his hands. I liked him holding me like that, but I wriggled my own hand away, ashamed because it looked so small and schoolgirlish. Two of my nails were broken right down, I'd picked a hangnail, and the writing lump on my middle finger was stained with ink.

'You'd like a hamburger, wouldn't you? I'd love to buy you a proper meal but there's not really time.'

'I don't want to cost you all this money,' I said shyly. 'You already paid me into the disco and then there were the drinks we had in there.'

'I'm earning, for Heaven's sake. And actually my Dad slipped me a fiver tonight just to make sure I wouldn't go short.'

'Your family sound ever so nice,' I said flatly.

'Well, they knew this evening was important for me,' said Richard, looking at me.

For a moment I didn't understand what he meant. Then I blushed. I knew it would be nice to tell Richard that the evening was important for me too, but I couldn't get the words out. I just smiled at him and ordered a hamburger too.

Chapter 5

We hurried down Waverton Parade and just as we arrived at the shop St Agatha's clock chimed the half-hour.

'How about that for perfect timing?' Richard said, laughing.

'Sh, don't talk so loud,' I whispered.

'Oh come on, Katy! Your Dad's not hiding behind the shop door eavesdropping, surely?'

'I wouldn't put it past him. He's got amazing hearing anyway. He always knows what you've mumbled behind his back. Sometimes he even hears what Nicola and I whisper when we're in bed. I think he must have ears like cartoon people – you know, they swell up and zoom out on stalks,' I giggled nervously. 'Well, I'd better go in now. Thanks for a really lovely time.' What if he tried to kiss me, right here in the shop doorway?

'Will you come out with me again?' said Richard.

'I – I'd like to, but it can't be much fun for you when I've got to be back so early. Are you sure you really want to?'

'Of course I want to. How about tomorrow, Saturday?'

'Oh no! I couldn't manage so soon. Dad would never believe me if I said my teacher had invited me round again.'

'Can't I see you in the day then? I don't always work on Saturdays.'

'I do though. I have to help in the shop.'

'I'll keep coming in the shop then, eh?'

'No! Oh Richard, you won't, will you? My Dad's so suspicious.'

'I'm getting a bit suspicious too. You're not just making up excuses not to see me, are you? I mean, if you are, just say so. It's all right, I won't burst into tears or fall prostrate at your feet.' He tried to turn it into a joke but his face was serious.

50

'I'm not inventing excuses, honestly.' I swallowed. 'I want to go out with you, Richard, really.'

'Good,' Richard whispered.

We stood looking at each other. It was too dark to see properly, but I was blushing and I was pretty sure Richard was too. I cleared my throat, ready to say a final goodbye, when Richard moved forward, bending his head. His lips touched the corner of my mouth, his cheek brushed mine, and then he moved back again quickly, because someone was coming along the parade. His cheek felt surprisingly soft and smooth.

'I must go in,' I whispered, as the man passed us. It was Mr Robertson from the bakery, walking his dog. He didn't seem to have noticed us, thank God.

'In a minute,' Richard whispered, and he put his arms round me properly.

This time he held me really close. I stood rigidly upright for a second or two, and then dared put my head against his chest. He gave a little grunt of appreciation and cuddled me.

'You feel so little,' said Richard. 'You're not much bigger than my kid sister Wendy, and she's only seven. Katy, when *am* I going to see you?'

'Tomorrow, when you do the newspaper round for Mark.'

'Yes, but that doesn't count. And he's coming back tomorrow night so he'll be doing the round himself on Sunday. What do you do on Sundays? Can't you make out you're going to church or something?'

'Maybe I could come out for a bit in the afternoon,' I said.

Dad shut the shop at lunch-time on Sundays. Mum roasted a meat loaf and veg for one o'clock and then Nicola and I washed up while Mum and Dad went to have a nap. Sometimes they didn't wake up until around four. Nicola and I were supposed to do our week-end homework or read quietly. Maybe I could slip out for an hour or so without Dad knowing.

'I'll wait at the bus stop then. What time?'

'About two? Only I mightn't be able to.'

'I'll wait.'

He bent and kissed me again, quickly.

'In you go then, Cinderella. See you Sunday,' he whispered.

I let myself in the side-door and stood in the dank passage

for a minute or two, trying to acclimatise myself. I could still feel the imprint of Richard's lips and cheeks and chest and arms, and when the feeling began to fade I stood in the dark hugging myself, trying to prolong the illusion. I didn't feel like myself any more. I might still be odd Katherine Petworthy in my school blouse, my sister's hair-ribbon and old jeans, but Richard had made me feel someone new and interesting and attractive.

I whirled up and down the passage, waltzing with myself. We still learnt Ballroom Dancing at Lady Margaret Lancaster's. Just think, I nearly didn't go out with Richard at all. It had been the most wonderful evening of my life. No, that sounded like a romantic magazine. What was I doing, galumphing about in the dark whispering clichés?

But I didn't want to be the old sneering critical Katherine any more. I *had* had a wonderful evening. All right, the disco had been rather an ordeal, and there had been awkward lapses in our conversation. But in spite of that we had got so close . . .

That's just it, I sneered. Close in more ways than one. You're making an idiot of yourself just because he kissed you.

But why not? I'd liked him kissing me so much. I'd had no idea it would be so lovely. It didn't really make me feel particularly passionate, certainly not the hot and fidgety feeling that occurred when I read a sexy passage in a book. I just felt warm and safe and cherished. I loved the feel of him, so strong and protective, and yet not at all clumsy or rough. His hands stroking my back had been so tender, as if I was very fragile and precious.

I couldn't remember anyone else ever holding me like that. Our family didn't go in for cuddles and kisses. Mum might have petted me a lot as a baby but she didn't cuddle me as I grew older. It wasn't really her fault. I knew I always wriggled away from her. She was too soft, too huge, too unresisting, a great rumpled unaired feather bed of a mother. I could remember wanting cuddles from Dad though, begging to be allowed to sit on his lap. Occasionally, when I'd been very clever indeed, Dad suffered my embraces, but always stiffly, as if I was getting him sticky or creased.

I could always cuddle Nicola of course. We had single beds but when we were little Nicola nearly always crept into mine.

She sometimes tried to curl up with me now, even though she was far too big for it to be practical. I sighed and moaned at her, but I didn't really mind. But it was just like cuddling Sniffle, Woffle and Muffle, comforting but not very exciting.

I wished I'd dared be a little more adventurous with Richard. I would have liked to try to kiss him back, to lift my hand and stroke his fluffy fair hair. Imagine his mother damping it down and brushing it back! I liked it when it flopped all over the place, I liked the way he flicked it out of his eyes every now and then, I liked the little duckling strands standing up at the crown of his head.

I wanted to stay in the passage thinking about him but it was getting later and later and I dreaded the day ending with a row. I forced myself upstairs, the unromantic smell of damp and kippers and cocoa getting stronger step by step.

'Is that you, Katherine?' Dad called sharply. 'Do you know the time? Keeping me up late like this, you've no consideration. What's got into you, staying out till this hour? What have you been up to, eh?'

I took a deep breath, feeling like an actress about to go on stage. Then I opened the door and walked into the living-room, forcing a smile.

'Sorry, Dad. Miss Hyde kept yacking on about Forster and Virginia Woolf and all these others, and I couldn't get away.'

'Where are all these books then? I thought she was going to –'

'She was so busy gassing she never really got round to lending me anything. She wants me to go back again soon,' I lied fluently.

'She's no business keeping you out this late. Schoolteachers ought to be a bit more responsible. I was just saying to your mother, five minutes more and then I was going to go out looking for you.'

'Oh *Dad*.' I imagined him walking swiftly towards Miss Hyde's dreary digs in Victoria Avenue, rapping indignantly at her front door, reeling back in alarm when Miss Hyde told him she had no idea where I was . . . But it hadn't happened, it was my lucky night and nothing could spoil it.

'Did she give you supper, dear, or would you like a little

snack? We've already had our cocoa, but I can make you a cup for yourself.'

'No thanks, Mum.'

'You're looking a bit flushed. Do you feel all right?' Mum asked, screwing her eyes up at me.

'Never mind Madam, it's me that's going to feel like grim death tomorrow. I'm the poor Joe that's got to get up at six o'clock sharp to sort those bally papers,' said Dad, getting up and switching off the television with a vicious tweak.

'Oh Dad, stop grumbling. Look, I'll set my alarm for tomorrow. I can easily do the papers myself. You have a lie in for once,' I said cheerily.

'Nice mess we'd be in then. You think it's so easy, but believe you me it's a job and a half. You think you know it all but –'

'Of course I do,' I said, laughing, and I caught hold of him while he was half off balance and twirled him round. 'The infant phenomenon, that's me.'

Nicola gasped, Mum froze in the act of hauling herself off the sofa, but Dad didn't explode.

'Now don't get above yourself,' he said shakily, pulling away from me, but his face was pink and looked almost pleased. He turned to Mum and Nicola. 'What's everyone gawping at? Come on, bed.'

'What's got into you?' Nicola whispered, as soon as we were in our bedroom together. 'The way you mucked about with Dad! And he didn't even get cross.'

I smiled enigmatically and started to get undressed. Mum had taught Nicola and me to dress and undress 'nicely'. That meant going through prudish contortions under our nighties. Nicola automatically poked her head through her blue brushed nylon and started undressing underneath. I normally behaved like a booby too, but tonight I felt more enterprising.

Softly humming 'The Stripper' I untied Nicola's hair ribbon with a flourish, whirled it around in the air, unbuttoned my blouse, simpering at each button, and then slipped my blouse off my shoulders, gyrating my minuscule breasts as best I could.

'Katherine!' Nicola squeaked, biting her lips to stop herself bursting out laughing. 'Kath, don't! You are *rude*.'

54

I became ruder, making a great play of unzipping my jeans and sliding them down my thighs. I pinged the sagging elastic on my baggy knickers, darting them down several inches. Then I turned my back, yanked everything off whilst imitating a great roll of drums, and grabbed Muffle. I turned round with a final flourish, totally naked, using Muffle like a fig leaf. Nicola snorted uncontrollably. I caught sight of myself in the mirror. Muffle was large and brown and furry. I looked as if I'd suddenly sprouted the most amazing luxuriant growth of pubic hair. I snorted too, collapsing on my bed. Nicola shook so much she staggered, tripped on the hem of her nightie, and fell groaning and gasping to the floor.

'What's all that noise in there?' Dad shouted. 'Stop the horseplay and get into bed, pronto, or I'll be in to sort you out.'

Weeping with silent laughter we did as we were told. Long after the light was out Nicola still shook with giggling fits.

'You didn't have anything to drink at Miss Hyde's did you?' she whispered.

'Only a double whisky. Oh, and a couple of sherries when I first got there.'

'Really?'

'Of course not, you nut.'

'Did you have anything to eat? She gave you Scotch pancakes last time, didn't she?'

'Do you really want to know what I had to eat tonight? I had a hamburger, not the awful gristly greasy things Mum cooks, but a proper meaty American hamburger in a sesame roll with pickle and relish and a blob of tomato sauce and a tiny little salad. It was delicious.'

'You're kidding, aren't you?' said Nicola.

'Maybe. Let's go to sleep. I'm tired.'

I wasn't tired at all, even though I'd woken up so early. I just wanted to lie quietly and think about Richard.

I dreamt about him too. An astonishing dream that made me blush when I woke up. I lay in a rosy stupor until Nicola leaned over to peer at my alarm.

'Oh cripes! We've slept in. It's nearly seven. Kath, get *up*. Dad will be going spare.'

I'd wanted to spend ages getting ready before seeing Richard, but now I couldn't even wash properly or brush my

55

hair. By the time we rushed down to the shop everyone else had left on their rounds. Dad was tight-lipped and terse.

'Thought you were getting up extra early, Madam? Get on with it, do. Nicola, push that hair back. Go on, both of you. I'm docking your pocket-money. You can't be late on your rounds and get off scot-free.'

Richard was outside, on his bike, waiting for me. My dream was still vivid and I knew I was blushing.

'Sleepyhead,' he said, grinning. 'I've been here ten minutes.'

Nicola stared.

'Go on, Nic, get cracking,' I said, giving her a push.

She looked at me, surprised.

'I'll see you back at the shop,' I said.

'Okay,' she said, walking off, but slowly, and turning round every now and then.

'I'll have to go too. Dad'll be mad if I'm late back.'

'How old's your sister? You can't be twins, you're not a bit alike, but – '

'She's only thirteen,' I said indignantly.

'You're obviously the runt of the family,' said Richard, and he reached out and patted my frizzy hair. I tried to jerk my head away but he caught hold of a strand and wound it round his finger.

'It's so springy,' he said.

'It's awful. In the lower school I had to wear a velour hat. Can you imagine! It kept jumping off my head even with elastic under my chin.'

'I like it. It's all fuzzy. I'll have to call you Fuzzypeg. Fuzzypeg was a sweet little hedgehog who – '

'I know. But I wouldn't have thought Little Grey Rabbit was your cup of tea,' I said, delighted.

'She's not. But I used to read some of those books to Wendy.'

'You don't half sound a nice brother.'

He shrugged. 'I just like little kids.'

'You don't! I hate them. And yet next week I've got to go to this awful nursery school on a work experience scheme.' I started moaning about it, until I glanced at Richard's watch and saw the time.

'Look at that! We've both got to get cracking! It's worse for

56

me, I've got Ladypark Close on my round, and if their *Times* and *Telegraphs* are ten minutes late they phone Dad up and complain.'

'Okay. Mind how you go. And remember two o'clock tomorrow.'

'Yes. I'll remember. Richard – do you really like my hair?'

He laughed and ruffled it with his hand.

'It's lovely and funny and different. Like you.'

All the way round Ladypark Close and Chestnut Drive and Springfield Avenue and Layton Gardens I sang 'Lovely and funny and different', running up paths, jumping over little gates, grinning wildly at every businessman and schoolchild and dog-walker.

I was much quicker than usual but Richard was back at the shop before me. We had another five minute conversation but then I saw Nicola lumbering into view at the other end of the Parade so I gave Richard's hand a quick squeeze and darted inside the shop. I even ate my breakfast sausages with relish.

Richard came into the shop three times that day, though he'd promised me he wouldn't. The first time Dad was there and glaring, so Richard quickly bought a box of fruit gums and went, giving me a wink as he passed. I didn't like that wink of his. It was silly and suggestive and Richard couldn't carry it off with the right air.

I spent the next hour wondering if he really was as nice as I'd begun to think. Then he came back again, just as Dad had gone upstairs to have a cup of tea and a ginger biscuit.

'Where's Mr Barrett?' he whispered.

It took me a second to realise who he meant and then I was delighted.

'Get you with your literary allusions! Fuzzypeg *and* Elizabeth and Robert.'

'There was an old film on the telly the other day, that's how I know about them. Sorry to disappoint you, but this is more my literary level,' he said, picking up a *Beano*. 'Where is your Dad anyway?'

'Having his elevenses.'

'But it's only half past ten.'

'That's typical of my Dad.'

'Still, I'm grateful for small mercies. How about having half past tensies with me? What do you fancy? Crisps and a can of coke? Bar of chocolate? I'm treating you. Last of the big spenders, that's me.'

I let him buy me a bar of Turkish Delight. Richard had a Yorkie.

'So I'm full of eastern promise and fluttering behind my veil while you're the big macho man flexing his muscles in his lorry,' I said. 'My sister and I used to play this game matching people to bars of chocolate. I said she was a Caramel bar, big and soft and sweet and oozy.'

'I don't think your sister thinks much of me. She doesn't half give me dirty looks.'

'I don't blame her,' I said, and dodged back behind the counter as he tried to swat me with the *Beano*. 'Hey, don't you crumple that or you'll have to pay for it.'

'I don't mind. I keep trying to wean Wendy onto it but she stays loyal to her *Twinkle*.'

I went over our conversation in my head at lunch, forking my way through my flacid plaice and boiled potatoes automatically.

'It's good to see you eating properly, girl,' Dad said suddenly, making me jump. 'You've got a bit of colour back in your cheeks. Here, perhaps I was a bit hasty this morning.' He put down his knife and fork and leant sideways to fumble in his pocket. 'Pocket-money time.'

'Thanks, Dad,' I said, pocketing my fifty pence.

Nicola sat still, chewing reproachfully. Dad picked up his knife and fork, and took a mouthful of potato, deliberately prolonging her agony, but as he swallowed he snapped his fingers as if he'd only just remembered. 'And you too, Nicola. Mustn't forget you. Here you are.'

'Come round the town with me, Kath?' Nicola whispered as we cleared the table and covered it with the green chenille cloth. Dad spread his accounts on the table. He said he spent Saturday afternoons balancing the books but he really watched 'Grandstand' on the television with the sound turned down very low. Mum served in the shop, and Nicola and I were free to do what we wanted for once.

'I don't really feel like it, Nic. We went round the town

58

yesterday, didn't we? No, I think I'll just stay in the shop and help Mum,' I said, trying to sound casual.

Nicola wrinkled her nose, puzzled. I had never volunteered to do a stint in the shop in my free time before.

'Why? What for? You hate serving in the shop. Kath, why are you being so mysterious? Stop keeping secrets from me, I hate it.'

'You can talk. Look at you, staying away from school all this time! You never breathed a word.'

'Sh! Oh Kath, don't!'

'It's all right, I'm not going to say anything. Just stop getting on to me. Go round the town by yourself.'

'But I'm always by myself. It's so much more fun with you. Kath, please. *Please.*'

She put her arm round me, nuzzling up hopefully. I wavered for a moment. Richard was very unlikely to come into the shop a third time – and after all, I'd told him not to. I rather wanted to go round the town myself. I was already worrying about what to wear on Sunday. I couldn't really wear my school blouse and jeans yet again. I certainly wasn't wearing the blue monstrosity, and that didn't leave much else. Maybe I'd be able to find a bargain in one of the charity shops. A skirt, a new blouse, even a pair of old stiletto heels. Or I could spend my pocket-money on a lipstick or mascara or eyeshadow – I couldn't really recommend Woolworth's watercolours as make-up.

But what if he *did* come back?

I sent Nicola off on her own and served in the shop. Mum wasn't particularly pleased.

'It's very nice of you, dear, but it's not really necessary. We'll just get under each other's feet.'

I sighed. She was obviously wanting a secret nosh at the sweets. She was usually just a great blur to me, but now I looked at her properly. Her hair was as wild and wiry as mine, but she screwed it up into a bun at the back of her neck and savaged it into submission with steel hairpins. Her face looked fatter than ever with her hair scragged back. Her eyes got lost in the great greasy mound of her face. It was as if a tiny blue-eyed woman was peering anxiously out of a grotesque mask. She looked such a *mess*. Her outsize polyester frock was

59

creased and there were stains under her arms. Her legs were bare because no stockings would fit those great fleshy pillars.

'What are you staring at?' she said uneasily.

'You haven't got your corset on.'

'I don't like to wear it when it's hot, it gets so uncomfortable.'

'You still ought to wear it. Look how your dress creases without it.'

'It brings me out in a rash.'

'You get that rash anyway. It's your skin rubbing against your skin, it's nothing to do with the corset. You look much better in it, Mum.'

'Look, I don't have to wear it, not if I don't want to,' she said, rearranging the magazines on the counter.

Whatever would Richard think if he came in and saw her? She was like a fairground exhibit.

'Mum, you look tired. Tell you what, why don't you go and have a lie down upstairs? I'll look after the shop this afternoon.'

'I'm not tired, dear. I'm fine.'

'Well, if I'm minding the shop you could go and have a little look round the town, maybe find Nicola and go round with her?'

'I don't want to! What is all this, Katherine?' said Mum – and just then Richard came into the shop.

He looked at Mum, then looked at me. I stared down at the bars of chocolate.

'Yes?' said Mum enquiringly.

Richard cleared his throat. 'A box of matches, please.'

Mum served him and took his money. I stayed looking at the counter, my eyes blurring. Richard turned to go and then hesitated.

'Mrs Petworthy?' he said to Mum.

I stared at him, horrified. He was red in the face, but smiling resolutely.

'I'm Richard, one of Katherine's friends. How do you do?'

He held out his hand to her. She blinked at him, extended her great salami sausage arm to shake his hand, and then realised she couldn't reach because of the birthday card display. She gave a flustered laugh and hurried to the gap in the

60

counter. Once there she forgot to edge herself sideways. She tried to rush it head-on and stuck fast.

We stood motionless, waiting. But Richard didn't snigger, rush away, or try to ignore what had happened.

'I think you'll have to back out again, Mrs Petworthy,' he said calmly. 'There's a counter like that at the printers where I work, and my Dad got stuck in it once. He's big too. He always says everything's designed for the little squirts in this world.'

Mum backed until her massive hips unplugged the counter. Richard reached over and clasped her hand.

'Pleased to meet you, Mrs Petworthy.'

She shook hands, still speechless.

'Cheerio then. See you, Katy.' He smiled at both of us and walked out of the shop.

Chapter 6

I knew I would need Nicola as an ally on Sunday afternoon so I decided to be very sweet to her in the morning. I suggested we play the Paper People game. Nicola gave a great whoop of joy and lugged the unwieldy book from her cupboard. It was a Style pattern book years out of date.

Mum had bought it cheaply from the dressmaking department of Rowbridge and Turner to inspire her when it came to making our clothes. She tried hard, copying a bow here, a kick-pleat there, with varying degrees of failure. Eventually we became so scathing that she gave up and used proper patterns. Nicola asked if she could have the book and cut out all the little fashion girls she could find with long, curly hair and party frocks. I watched her snip one particularly simpering specimen and decided to give her a personality. She became Patty Pert, eight years old, cosseted only daughter of Bert and Gert Pert, publican and wife. Patty was a doyen of her local dancing class, had once acted in a television commercial for toilet paper and was determined to further her career in show business.

Nicola was mildly annoyed at first because she wanted her to be called something wetly romantic like Miranda or Arabella, but after a while she became fond of Patty. She mounted her on cardboard so that every little Pert fingernail and ringlet stayed intact and asked me to make up a friend for her.

Now, years later, we had a cardboard cast of at least fifty favourites, with another hundred or so paper people for crowd scenes. Nicola had her own little group of girls who were sometimes pupils at a stage school, sometimes orphans in a very bleak orphanage, sometimes rich cousins living in an enormous mansion in the country. She had her way with their names: as well as Miranda and Arabella there were Samantha, Alicia, Michaela, Clarissa, Pandora and Anastasia.

My own paper people were glamorous women inappropriately christened Charlotte, Emily, Anne, Virginia, Sylvia, Marianne and Jane. They were all elaborately dressed for dancing, but there was a shortage of paper partners apart from a few old faithfuls from the menswear section and a couple of precocious schoolboys. I had to help out by inventing my own men, some dashing, some dreary. One day when I was bored I made up a fumbly little man in a greasy raincoat to lurk near my paper ladies. I was rather fond of Mr Tremble but Nicola said he made her feel sick, and when he started to edge up to pretty Patty Pert she banished him to the back of the fashion book.

Sometimes we organised a birthday party or a special outing for the Paper People, sometimes we concentrated on one little group, sometimes we invented an interesting disaster. Mr Tremble disgraced himself several times and was tried and sent to prison. Miranda, Arabella etc., once had a sister called Araminta who contracted a fatal illness, languished for an interminable time, and then eventually died so movingly that Nicola was in floods of tears and Mum asked me what on earth I'd been doing to upset poor Nicola so much.

But these set piece scenes were all former glories. It was becoming more and more difficult to invent new happenings. I was sick of every single one of the paper people. Nicola never minded repeating a game, making the characters go over the same scenes, but it made me want to scream with boredom.

This Sunday Nicola wanted to play schools with Miranda and Co yet again, and set them out lovingly on our bedroom carpet, finding all the crumpled little props, the paper books and pens, the paper cane, the paper stool and dunce's cap.

'Now, let's play the game where Pandora's the new girl and Miss Paisleyprint is horrible to her but Miss Floralsmock comes along and is all nice and comforting,' said Nicola happily.

'Not again, Nic. Let's try to think of something new. I know, Miss Floralsmock looks a bit tubby, doesn't she? Perhaps she's pregnant. Who can the father be? Perhaps she was attacked in the school grounds by Mr Tremble and – '

'No! Not him. Stop making it all horrible. Miss Floralsmock is not pregnant.'

'Oh go on, Nic, look, we could find her a baby.'

I turned to the baby section of the fashion book. They were about the only pages left uncut.

'There's heaps of the little beasts here. Select an infant Floralsmock. We won't have Mr Tremble for a Daddy. Miss Floralsmock has had a very romantic passionate affair with Derek Dressing-gown. Now, you don't mind him, do you? He's very dashing and he's got such a kind smile. I tell you what, we'll make it thoroughly respectable. First we will engineer the romance. Then we will have a wedding, and all your silly girls can be bridesmaids. Then we will have a decent interval and then Miss Floralsmock will start to swell beneath her fetching little smock and *then* she can give birth to her very own little . . . what's a diminutive for Floralsmock? Budbib! Oh, Budbib, yes. Come here, Nic, help me find a perfect Budbib. What about this one? It's fat like Miss Floralsmock and fair like Derek Dressing-gown.'

Nicola warmed to the idea of a wedding. She got an old Sunday Times colour supplement and chose presents for the happy pair, while I drew a jolly vicar to join Miss Floralsmock and Derek Dressing-gown in holy matrimony. Nicola insisted that they have a proper reception which took an interminable time, but I enjoyed helping them consumate their marriage. Nicola got very red and giggly and kept telling me I wasn't half *rude*. After all that passion it wasn't long before little Budbib was on the way. I made Miss Floralsmock pant and shriek her way through a traumatic labour while ineffectual old Derek fainted dead away. I changed the vicar into a doctor who delivered the baby efficiently and Miss Floralsmock recovered enough to be holding the infant in a Madonna pose by the time Derek Dressing-gown regained consciousness.

I was getting tired of the game by this time, but Nicola wanted to continue playing with Budbib, pretending to feed him and change his nasty little nappy and put him to sleep. I started to think about the Lingfield Road nursery school tomorrow. What would I say to all those strange little children? Would I have to try to make them do things? I could lord it over Budbib and Patty Pert and all the others, but I was useless with real flesh and blood children. My stomach clenched uneasily as I thought about it. I tried to comfort myself in the usual way, telling myself that it didn't matter that I was so odd and different. It was simply because I was gifted and nearly everyone with very high IQs had difficult childhoods. But then I couldn't stop myself remembering the O level exams and I was felled with further doubts.

'Kath?' Nicola looked up from Budbib and stared at me, wrinkling her nose. 'Kath, you're nearly crying!'

'Of course I'm not. Don't be stupid,' I snapped. 'I'm just fed up with this game. I've been playing for hours and hours.'

I started moodily sorting through my wardrobe, desperate to find some alternative to my jeans and old T-shirt to wear to meet Richard. The T-shirt was tight and cruelly exposed my ten year old's chest. I didn't know what to do. If I left my bra off the only part of me that stuck out were my two tiny nipples; if I wore my bra then there were just two silly ruches of material instead of breasts. I picked up my discarded school shirt and had a quick smell under the arms. No, it was definitely too sweaty to wear again. In desperation I held the blue monstrosity against me to see if it was really as bad as I feared. It was worse.

'What are you getting that dress out for? It looks awful,' said Nicola tactlessly.

'All right, but it's going to look even worse on you, you great fat lump.'

Nicola stared at me, stricken, her eyes filling with tears.

'I'm sorry, I'm sorry, I didn't mean it,' I said quickly. 'Don't take any notice of me, Nic, I'm just fed up. Leave me alone for a bit, eh?'

Nicola quickly gathered up the Paper People and tucked them inside the front cover.

'Anyway, thanks ever so much for playing with me, Kath. It's been a simply marvellous morning. You are good to me.'

She went downstairs leaving me feeling dreadful. I wasn't good to her at all, I was often hateful. It was so tempting to take things out on her. I felt a sick sense of recognition whenever Dad started torturing her.

I turned on my stomach, burrowing my head hard into my pillow, hating myself so much I wanted to escape into darkness. But I couldn't burrow for ever. What was I going to do when the envelope came with my O level results? What was I going to do? What was I going to do? *What was I going to do?*

'Exams aren't everything, are they?'

I stopped squirming on the bed and lay still. Richard. I whispered his name several times, rolling him round my tongue as if he were a boiled sweet. Not the silly Richard with the wink and the slicked back hair and the borrowed jacket. The sweet, kind, gentle Richard who had treated my mother with such aplomb.

I wondered what Mum would say if I told her I was meeting Richard this afternoon. She might not mind too much but she would be terrified of Dad finding out. It was much simpler to keep quiet about it to everyone.

I sat up and looked down at my flat front. Those boys in the shop had laughed and said I had no tits at all. The girls at school teased me too, and Maggie Turner had started a ridiculous rumour that I was really a boy and hadn't anyone else noticed the suspicious lump in Katherine's knickers when she did gym? That was cleverly cruel of her, because once a month I really did have a lump in my gym knickers. I wasn't allowed to use Tampax like everyone else. Mum said she didn't think it was healthy, and when I bought a packet for myself out of my precious pocket money she came barging into my room and confiscated them. I was stuck with awful old sanitary towels and had to suffer all those nudges and winks every month when we had games.

I sighed and peered down inside the neck of my T-shirt.

'Grow, can't you?' I muttered.

I didn't want to go to extremes. I didn't care for huge melons, the sort that pin-up girls paraded. (Dad wouldn't stock any girlie magazines at all, not even *Playboy* or *Penthouse*. He said soft porn or hard porn, they were all muck, and he wasn't having them in his shop, thank you very much). I would have been happy with small, shapely breasts, little apples. Mine were barely cherries.

But maybe Richard wasn't like those hateful boys that came into the shop. Maybe he didn't care about the size of my breasts. After all, he hadn't seemed to mind at all about Mum's hugeness. If he was indifferent to her abundance of flesh then

66

maybe he was equally indifferent to my lack of it. And what was the matter with me anyway, making such a mountain out of two minute molehills?

I giggled and jumped off the bed. It must be nearly lunch-time. The smell of meatloaf was getting stronger. It had a particularly rich and disgusting smell, like unwashed armpits. I wondered why on earth Mum always had to cook such pungent food.

Mum and Dad went to have their nap after lunch while Nicola and I tackled the dishes. We usually argued over who had to Vim out the disgusting meatloaf tin and all the slimy vegetable pots, but I did them all, even though I had done them last time too.

'There,' I said, when it was all finished. I looked round the room as if I was trying to think what to do next. I shifted my weight from my heels to my toes, and hummed.

'I think I might go for a little walk,' I announced.

Nicola said she would come too. I said I wanted to be by myself. Nicola persisted and I had to get fierce.

'Why are you being so horrible to me?' Nicola said plaintively.

'I'm not! I've been extra specially nice to you today. I spent hours playing Paper People with you, I did nearly all the washing up myself – '

'I never asked you to. Anyway, you can't stop me coming with you.'

'Oh don't be ridiculous. I'm going now.'

'So am I.'

Nicola followed me right down the stairs and out of the door. I thought she was bluffing, but she followed me along the pavement.

'Nicola, you're being absolutely childish! Go away. Look, you've still got your slippers on.'

'I don't care.'

'Well, I do. I'm not walking down the road with you like that. Now go straight home. You haven't even got a key. Here's mine. Mind you let me in when I come back.'

'I'm coming with you,' said Nicola.

'No you are *not*.'

I started running and she ran too, grabbing hold of my arm.

67

I swung away from her furiously and pushed her so hard she nearly fell over.

'Will you leave go of me, you great fat pig. You are not tagging along with me. If you must know I'm going to meet my boy-friend. He certainly wouldn't want you trailing round with us. So go *home*.'

Nicola burst into tears and dashed back to the shop. I went on walking along Waverton Parade, my heart beating twice as fast as usual, my T-shirt sticking to my back. I tried to feel triumphant, but my throat ached and I knew I might easily burst into tears myself.

Richard was waiting for me at the bus-stop as we had arranged. He was standing with his arm round a little girl. His sister.

Wendy was licking an ice lolly and holding a large baby doll in her arms. She was like a doll herself. She had big blue eyes with long, curling lashes that looked as if they might open and shut with a click. Her little pursed mouth was artificially red with lolly stains. Her skin looked plastic, pink and shiny. Her hair was so fair it was almost white. She wore it in two long, smooth plaits secured with cherry bobbles to match her red checked dress. She seemed big for seven, a great glossy child-size doll.

'Hello Katy,' said Richard. He looked at me carefully. 'What's up?'

'Nothing,' I mumbled.

'You didn't mind me bringing Wendy, did you?' said Richard.

'Of course not.' I nodded jerkily to Wendy. 'Hello, Wendy.'

Wendy didn't reply. She sucked violently at her lolly and took a step closer to Richard.

'Say "hello" then,' said Richard. He smiled at her indulgently. 'She's a bit shy.'

Wendy didn't seem shy to me. Her blue eyes flickered over me. She didn't look impressed. Red water from her ice lolly trickled up her arm, staining the wrist of her white cardigan.

'Wendy! Watch out, you mucky thing. Mum'll go spare if you get that all over your cardi,' said Richard, dabbing at her with a handkerchief.

Wendy licked the drips away. Her pointed tongue was

68

stained deep crimson. She waggled it at me as Richard bent over her. I stuck my own tongue out as far as it would go. Wendy looked faintly surprised.

'I usually take Wendy to Dudhope Park on Sundays. Is that all right with you, Katy?' said Richard.

'Yes.'

I had only been in Dudhope Park half a dozen times in my life although it was only ten minutes' walk from Waverton Parade. Dad had taken me there to feed the ducks when I was little. It was supposed to be a great treat but Dad was determined to make the outing educational, and kept firing questions at me. He asked me the number of swings and then got me to subtract two and then add six, but he told me to stop whining when I begged to go on one. He asked me to count the trees at the top of the hill and asked what happened to the green leaves in the winter but he told me to stop messing about when I zigzagged through the trees and started running down the hill pretending to fly.

I could only remember once going to the park with Nicola. She was still in her pushchair. It was a damp winter's day and she was huddled inside a hideous red plastic coverall, her pale face peering out anxiously every now and then. We ignored her until we got to the duckpond. I had given her the paper bag of bread to hold on her lap, but when I tried to recover it the bag was empty, apart from a few crumbs. Dad lost his temper and smacked Nicola hard for eating the bread. She cried passionately and I cried too, because I couldn't feed the ducks, and Dad ranted at us all the way home and said he would never take us to the bally park again. He kept his word. Mum didn't ever take us, of course. She would never go out unless she had an unavoidable reason, like shopping. She was always worried people would stare at her because she was so fat. Nicola and I didn't try to persuade her. We knew people did stare, and we hated it.

'Hey, there is something wrong, isn't there?' said Richard.

Wendy had finished her ice lolly and hung on to him with one sticky hand, but he gently detached himself and turned to me. Wendy marched on ahead, her red sandals squeaking, muttering to her doll.

'I had a bit of a row with my sister,' I said.

69

'What was it about?'

'Oh, nothing really. I'm just horrible to her sometimes. I'm horrible to everyone.'

'Not to me.'

'You don't know me properly.'

'Yes I do.' He reached out and put his arm round me, pulling me close.

'Richard! Wendy will see,' I whispered.

'So what? I'm so glad you came. I was worried in case I might have got you into trouble. You know, introducing myself to your mother.'

I grew hot. 'You were very . . . Anyway, it's Dad who won't let me do anything, not Mum.'

'But he let you come out this afternoon? You didn't spin another yarn about seeing a schoolteacher, did you?'

'No. It's all right, Mum and Dad have a nap for a couple of hours on Sunday afternoons.'

'Do they?' said Richard, looking amused.

'Yes, I don't know why. Perhaps meat loaf is particularly soporific. They always have a nap, Sunday after Sunday after Sunday.'

'Are you pulling my leg?'

'What?'

'You know why they have their so-called nap?'

'Because they're tired.'

'Oh Katy, you are sweet.'

I was beginning to get irritated. I couldn't see what he was getting at. Why else would Mum and Dad go up to bed? And then it dawned on me, and I blushed.

'No, it's not that!' I protested. 'My parents – they wouldn't. They're too old.'

'Of course they're not,' said Richard.

'But you can't possibly imagine – Richard, you've seen my mother. They don't do it.'

'How do you think you and Nicola got here then? You can't kid me you're adopted, you've got your Mum's hair and your Dad's build.'

'That's bad enough, but thank goodness it wasn't the other way round,' I said quickly.

Richard looked surprised. 'Don't be nasty.'

70

'I told you I could be horrible.'

'Oh well, horrible or not, I still like you,' said Richard, giving me a squeeze. 'Hey, Wendy, don't cross the road by yourself. Wait for us.'

Wendy wanted to go to the children's playground just inside the park gates. It was a dull little patch of asphalt unimaginatively sprinkled with swings, roundabout, a rickety slide and a sand-pit. Wendy rushed about as enthusiastically as if it was Disneyland.

'Watch me, Richard! Watch me!' she shrieked, hurling herself down the slide with her short skirt flying, the baby doll hanging queasily over the edge.

Richard watched patiently, and then pushed Wendy for an interminable time on the swings. I wandered over to the roundabout. I sat on it and pushed it slowly with one plimsoll, going round inch by inch. I thought about Mum and Dad in bed. Could Richard be right? Were they grappling on their yellow candlewick right this minute? It was so hard to imagine. I couldn't even get their clothes off. I knew Dad wore old string vests and pants because they flapped weekly on the washing line but I'd never actually seen him in his underwear. When he rolled the sleeves of his shirt up in hot weather his arms looked very pale and hairless and exposed, as if he'd peeled back an extra skin by mistake. I imagined his whole body waxy pale and pathetic behind the ludicrous lattice of his underwear. And Mum, oh God, Mum. Which was worse? Mum controlled in her salmon corset, her huge breasts rearing up to her chin and her belly punched into submission – or Mum exploded from the corset, great globes of quivering flesh and a silly little thatch roofing her rude bit?

No, they'd never make love stark naked. If they did it at all then they'd do it in their night things and under cover of the bedclothes. But how would they manage it with Mum twice the size of Dad? I tried to remember the different positions I'd glimpsed in the sex book one of the girls had smuggled to school. Presumably Dad would have to perch on top of Mum . . . No, it was just too ridiculous.

'What are you thinking about?' Richard joined me on the roundabout.

'Oh, nothing.'

71

'You're blushing.'

'I know. I'm always doing it. I hate it.'

'It looks pretty,' said Richard, touching my burning cheek. 'Do I embarrass you then, Katy?'

'No. No, you don't,' I said.

'Good.' He stroked my cheek gently with the back of his fingers.

'I can't get over how soft girls' cheeks are.'

'Your skin's soft too. You shave, don't you?'

'Of course I do!'

'I don't know much about boys, when they start shaving, and all the rest of it.'

'Am I the first boy you've been out with?'

'Yes,' I admitted, feeling foolish.

But Richard looked delighted.

'I thought so.'

'Presumably you've been out with other girls?'

'Bevies of them,' said Richard. 'Well, a few. I went steady with one girl for six months but then that just fizzled out.'

'Do you think we'll fizzle?' I said.

'You might, but I won't,' said Richard. 'I can't imagine getting fed up with you. You're so different from other girls.'

I shook my head. 'Don't. I don't want to be different.' I hesitated. 'Remember what you said about my hair?'

'Of course I do.'

'What, then?' I said suspiciously.

'It's lovely and funny and different. Like you.'

I grinned. 'You did remember.'

'See,' said Richard, and he bent his head and kissed me, half on my lips, half on my cheek.

Wendy, abandoned on her swing, made raucous noises.

'Look at the love-birds!' she jeered.

'Take no notice,' said Richard and kissed me again, slowly and deliberately, his lips properly on mine.

I felt as if the roundabout was spinning faster and faster, up into the air, right up above the tall poplars at the edge of the playing fields.

Chapter 7

Wendy shouted abuse. When her voice cracked miserably Richard sighed and we broke apart.

'I'll give her another push,' he said, but she sprang from her swing.

'I want to go in the sand-pit,' she said. 'Come on, Richard, come over there with me.'

Wendy was too old for the sand-pit. Richard protested and teased her a little, but in the end we sat at the edge while Wendy squatted self-consciously in the sand-pit. A little girl of about two was in the sand-pit already, her white knickers stained yellow with sand. She held a red, plastic spade and stuck it happily but uselessly in her patch of sand again and again.

'Do you want to lend me your spade, little girl?' said Wendy.

The little girl stared at her doubtfully. Wendy looked as if she might take silence as acquiescence, but the little girl's mother was sitting on a bench nearby and looked fierce.

'I can't build a castle without a spade,' Wendy whined.

'Use a big stone or a carton or something,' Richard suggested, busy burying my plimsolled feet in the sand.

Wendy tried for a few seconds, and then hurled the paper cup she'd found to the other end of the pit. The little girl squeaked with surprise, and her mother looked up and frowned at Wendy.

'It won't work,' Wendy wailed. 'Richard, you do it for me. Make me a castle.'

'What it is to be in demand,' I said, as Richard sighed and stood up.

'She's not usually all babyish and whiny like this,' said Richard.

He knelt beside Wendy and scooped up sand so that she

could pat it into shape. I sat at the edge of the pit, watching them. Wendy's doll lay abandoned, head in the sand, limbs splayed pathetically. I picked her up and blew the sand off her. She was naked apart from a grubby nappy and a fraying bib. Her hair was thinning in parts and very dishevelled. I combed it with my fingers and repinned the drooping nappy.

'She's got my doll,' Wendy complained.

'I'm sorting her out for you. She fell into the sand. What's her name?'

'Madeleine, after my best friend at school.'

'How old is she?'

'My friend? Seven, like me,'

'No, your doll Madeleine.'

'She's a baby,' said Wendy.

'Yes, but she must have an age. Can she talk at all yet? Can she crawl? Does she try to feed herself?'

Wendy stopped patting her castle and screwed up her face at Richard.

'She's mad,' she said.

It was always the same. I could never get on with children. She thought I was mad.

'Don't be so cheeky or I'll smash your castle,' Richard said sternly. He raised his eyebrows at me. It was still Richard and me against Wendy.

'I am mad,' I said suddenly. 'I keep it under control most of the time but sometimes it breaks out, especially when there's a full moon. It's coming up to full moon time now, Wendy. By this evening I shall start talking complete gibberish, addressing all sorts of inanimate objects. "Hello table," I'll say. "How do, chair." But they haven't got mouths to answer me back. I'm too old for my own dolls but I'll remember yours. I'll decide to come and have a chat with her. I'll stagger along the streets to your house, utterly demented, mopping and mowing, drooling down my chin –' I hunched up hideously and pulled appropriate faces, making Wendy shriek, 'and I'll batter at your door, demanding to come and talk to Madeleine. You might think you can lock the door and keep me out, but I'll climb up the drain-pipe right up to your bedroom and I'll tap at your window and you'll wake up and see my distorted, mad face mouthing at you behind the glass and –'

'She's making it up, isn't she, Richard?' said Wendy uncertainly.

I pulled the face again and she screamed appreciatively. The little girl's mother saw me, leapt to her feet, removed her daughter from the sand-pit, and carried her to safety.

Richard and Wendy and I grinned at each other.

'Oh dear, she's left her spade behind,' said Wendy delightedly. 'Do that face again, Katy, I like that mad face.'

'Don't you really know how old Madeleine is? Wouldn't you be shocked if your mother had no idea how old you are?'

'Yes, but Madeleine's only a doll,' said Wendy. 'She wets after you give her a bottle. She's got a special little hole.'

'What's so special about that? Can't she do anything else yet? Shall I teach her to crawl?'

I made Madeleine wriggle inexpertly in the sand.

'Nearly. Nearly. That's the way, my dear. Yes – ooh!' I let her fall on her face. 'Never mind. Let's rub that nose better then. Now, try again. Show Wendy you're more than a wee-wee machine.'

Wendy chuckled. 'I forgot, she cries too.'

'I'd cry, if my mother was so neglectful. Look, she's crawling properly now. The sand-pit must seem like the Sahara desert to her. Let's make her a little oasis. Those lolly sticks could be tiny, stunted trees, and if you bury that coke can until just the top shows it'll look a bit like a pond.'

We played with Madeleine for a while, and when we left the sand-pit Wendy held my hand as well as Richard's.

'I didn't know big girls played with dolls, but you aren't half good at it, Katy,' she said.

'Katy's not a big girl, she's nearly as little as you,' said Richard, smiling at me over Wendy's head.

We walked round by the duck pond, over the playing-fields, and around the ornamental flower beds. They were predictably patriotic, salvias and geraniums, alyssum and lobelia. Wendy shook herself free of us and ran round the largest flower-bed three times because Richard told her she would get a wish if she did.

'We'll do it too,' he said, pulling me round.

We ran, faster and faster, until when we stopped I had to

cling to Richard, while the red, white and blue flowers whirled on independently.

'Wish, go on, wish, Katy,' Richard said.

I shut my eyes and my thoughts were in a whirl too. I nearly wished something to do with Richard until I remembered my O levels. Then, of course, there was no alternative. I wished that a miracle would happen and I would pass all eleven at A grades.

'I wished!' Wendy shouted. 'Shall I tell you what I wished, Richard?'

'You mustn't tell your wish or it won't come true,' I said.

'Oh no, that's only if you run round anticlockwise,' said Richard quickly. 'We all ran clockwise, so we *have* to tell our wishes. If we keep them secret then they won't come true.'

Wendy was artful too. 'Okay, then I wished for a big 99 ice-cream, and look, there's an ice-cream stall over there, see.'

'You monkey,' said Richard, pretending to pull her plaits. 'You've only just had that ice lolly. You'll never eat tea, and Mum will nag at me.'

'Yes I will so eat tea, it's trifle, and I'll have a double portion, you just wait and see. *Can* I have an ice-cream, Richard?'

'Yes, all right. You'll have one, won't you, Katy?'

'Please.' I thought guiltily of Nicola again. She was passionately fond of whippy ice-creams. I could have asked her along too, Richard wouldn't have minded. Although I would. I didn't want silly old Nicola lumbering around with us.

'What did you wish, Katy?' said Richard, as we walked over to the ice-cream stall.

'Never you mind.'

'You've got to tell or it won't come true. Come on. Tell. Please.' He looked at me eagerly, his brown eyes shining. What did he think I'd wished?

'All right then. I wished I'd done well in my O levels,' I said truthfully.

'No you didn't!'

'I did. I swear I did.'

'What a boring wish,' said Richard, disappointed.

'I love the way you don't give a damn about exams,' I said. 'What did you wish then, Richard?'

'Never you mind,' he said, imitating me.

76

'Oh come on!'

'Well, I didn't wish about exams.'

'I know that.'

'And I didn't wish for an ice-cream.'

'So what did you wish for?'

But Richard broke away from me and ran back to the flower-bed, running round it anticlockwise this time.

'Now I can't tell you,' he said.

'You're a cheat.'

'No, he's not,' said Wendy. 'But he always manages to win. It isn't half annoying. Every single time we've ever played "Monopoly" or "Snakes and Ladders" or anything, he wins. Can I have strawberry sauce on my ice-cream as well as a 99, Richard?'

There was a long queue at the ice-cream van. Wendy hopped and skipped beside Richard, while I went to sit on a bench. There was an old woman at the other end of the bench. She was hunched into her fur coat although it was summer and very warm. It was a musquash coat, brittle with age, the marmalade wisps of fur dark grey at the roots, like old dyed hair. Her own hair was hidden under a ragged chiffon scarf. She'd tried to tie the fraying ends in a knot so that they wouldn't show. She wore boots, stubby old-lady zip-up boots, but her thin legs were bare. She sensed me looking and quickly tried to tuck them under the bench.

It was a shock realising that she minded her grey legs and ugly boots. Her lips were moving although she didn't make any noise. Nicola said my own lips moved eerily whenever I was making things up inside my head. Perhaps the old woman was having an imaginary conversation.

She looked up suddenly and our eyes met. I felt a thrill of terror as she stared at me, a nerve twitching in her rouged cheek. She looked as if she recognised me. Would I end up like her one day, mad and grubby and totally alone?

Richard came back with a huge ice-cream for me, great white peaks smothered in strawberry sauce, with a glacé cherry on top. The ice-cream glistened in the sunlight. It looked so perfect it seemed an act of sacrilege to plunge my tongue into its midst. Richard and Wendy were already licking busily.

The old woman watched us. She was looking at my ice-cream.

Richard and Wendy walked on ahead, chattering. I hesitated and then I thrust my ice-cream into the old woman's freckled hand.

It was a mistake. I expected her to be grateful. But she sat holding the ice-cream stiffly in front of her, not responding. It started to melt in the sunlight, dripping onto her moulting fur. She watched it drip and then she suddenly jerked her arm feebly and threw my beautiful ice-cream onto the ground, amongst the bird droppings and cigarette stubs.

Wendy was horrified. Even Richard seemed baffled.

'Don't you like ice-cream, Katy?'

'Yes, I love it. But I thought she'd like it. I didn't think she'd just throw it away,' I said miserably.

'I'll buy you another then. Or look, have the rest of mine.'

'I don't want one now, Richard, honestly. I'm sorry. You didn't mind me giving it to her, did you?'

'No, of course not,' said Richard.

'It cost 40p, that ice-cream,' said Wendy sternly. 'What a waste.'

I couldn't explain to them why I'd given my ice-cream away. I wasn't really sure myself. The enjoyment of being in the park with Richard melted as fast as the ice-cream. I told them I had to go home. I wanted to get away from them but Richard insisted on walking me right back down Waverton Parade to the front door. Wendy stared at us stonily once we had got there. It was impossible to kiss in front of her. Richard's head jerked forward once or twice, but it stopped before it reached me. In the end he just squeezed my hand.

'Good luck tomorrow, at the school. I bet you'll find you enjoy yourself,' he said.

I smiled wanly, not bothering to argue. I waited for him to suggest another meeting. I had decided to risk the Miss Hyde alibi once more. But Richard didn't ask me to go out with him again. He said goodbye and walked off with Wendy hopping beside him, Madeleine trailing from one hand.

I'd thought he was so keen on me. He obviously didn't think me so lovely now. I was just funny and different, and he'd had enough of me.

I trailed upstairs. Nicola was hunched up in the armchair doing nothing. Her eyes were very red.

At least Mum and Dad were still safely in their bedroom either having a nap or having each other. The slick turn of phrase sounded peculiar, as if Mum and Dad were tucking into each other, nibbling a toe or two, gnawing at a crunchy shin, slavering over a slice of juicy rump. Mum would make a gargantuan meal for Dad, but he'd be a very stringy morsel.

'Nicola, what's the name of that weird insect that chomps up its sexual partner? A praying something or other.'

Nicola shrugged indifferently.

'You're the one who's meant to know everything,' she mumbled.

She sat with her knees up in the armchair, her head lolling.

'Nic, I'm sorry I was so horrible to you. I didn't mean what I said, you know I didn't,' I said, going over to her.

I was going to scoop her up in my arms and give her a hug. But when I got near enough I hung back. She smelt so sweaty for a start. She had probably been crying a lot, that always made her smell. We shared a stick of deodorant but it never seemed to work effectively for Nicola. I saw the damp crescents under the arms of her T-shirt. Her face looked damp too, her nose shining, her eyelids raw. Why couldn't she wash herself, for God's sake? Why did she have to slummock there, so sourly pathetic?

'Come on, don't sulk,' I said, sitting on the arm of the chair.

'I'm not rotten well sulking,' Nicola mumbled, tears gathering in her eyes again.

'I've said I'm sorry, what more can I say? I just got mad because you would keep tagging on. You've got to understand, Nic. We can't go round everywhere together.'

'You called me a big fat pig,' Nicola said sorrowfully.

'I didn't mean it.'

'That's what you always say. Afterwards. You think you've got the perfect right to say the most hateful things, and then you expect everyone to forgive you and forget all about it just because you say you didn't mean it. Well I'm sick of it, sick of you bossing me about and telling me what to do. And what do you mean, you've got a boy-friend? Why didn't you tell me?

It's not Mark's friend, is it? The boy who did the newspaper round?'

'Never you mind! And do stop shouting. They'll be coming down any minute.'

'Oh yes, that's the only reason you want to make friends with me, just so you won't get into trouble,' said Nicola, scrubbing at her eyes with a sodden handkerchief.

'You know perfectly well that if anyone gets into trouble it will be you,' I said cruelly. 'Dad can't bear it when you cry.'

'I'm not crying,' Nicola sobbed, stuffing the handkerchief down the arm of the chair and using the hem of her skirt instead.

'Go and wash your face. You're just making it worse.'

'You stop telling me what to do. I won't stand for it,' Nicola shouted, and ran to the bathroom.

I was left in the stale little living-room. I wandered backwards and forwards across the worn carpet. I hit the ugly black leatherette of the armchair so hard that dust exploded into the air. I wanted to smash every stick of shoddy furniture, every ornament in the cabinet. I wanted to rip up the kitten calendar and the carrot-coloured painting of woods in autumn. I wanted to tear the hideous wipe-clean wallpaper from the walls. I hated my home. I hated my family. I hated myself.

It wasn't fair. I wanted to be nice to Nicola but it was so difficult when she looked such a mess and said such stupid things. It was so much easier for Richard with pert, pretty little Wendy. I thought of them both, so fair, so clear-skinned, so clean. If Nicola washed her hair more frequently and brushed it properly then it might look nearly as nice as Wendy's. She couldn't help her clothes, but she could stop stuffing herself with food so that she didn't look so lumpy. She'd end up like Mum if she wasn't careful.

But what about me? Would I end up like Dad, small-minded and sadistic, venting my spite on my family? Or wouldn't I have a family at all? Would I be like the woman in the park?

Chapter 8

I knew it was stupid to be so scared. I pretended that I would be perfectly all right when I got there. I tried to imagine myself amusing a lot of little Wendys, making their dolls talk, pulling funny faces, telling them stories. But as I went through the gate and up the asphalt path to the ugly little redbrick nursery I had to stand still, praying that I wasn't going to be sick in front of all the mothers and children.

The mothers were very assorted. Some were granny age, in lemon or turquoise crimplene frocks and flat plastic sandals. Others looked barely older than me, rushing around in tight jeans and T-shirts. There were a couple of tarty mothers with very short skirts and very high heels, and a lot of earnest earth mothers in patchwork and limp Laura Ashley. The children all looked the same. Terrifying.

One ugly little girl in skimpy shorts that showed her knickers sat down in the middle of the path, clutching her mother's ankles.

'I want to go home!' she wailed, her eyelashes spiky with tears.

I felt like wailing it too. I forced myself inside the door and stood in the little cloakroom, wondering where to go.

'Is she a mother or a little girl?' a small boy asked his mother.

'She's a big girl, silly.'

I decided to try hard.

'I'm a helper,' I said. I bent towards him until our faces were a foot apart. He had Ribena stains round his mouth and he smelt of stale bedclothes, but I was determined to be friendly. 'What's your name then?'

He backed away from me anxiously.

'Gavin! Tell the big girl your name,' said Gavin's mum, giving him a little shake.

81

Gavin remained mute.

'Kids!' said Mum. 'Come on then, Gavin, are you going to paint me a picture this morning?'

'I don't like that big girl,' Gavin announced loudly as they walked off.

I stared at the row of brightly coloured pictures above the red pegs. An apple, a bear, a chair, a dog, an elephant . . .. . They started to blur.

'Katherine Petworthy!'

I blinked and turned round. Louise Joplin and Maggie Turner were standing there, staring at me. They were in Upper V alpha too. They were both wearing jeans. Oh God. I had dressed automatically in my school uniform.

'Didn't Mrs Philpotts tell you? We don't have to wear uniform?' said Louise.

She wasn't so bad, a tall, thin, giggly girl with floppy Princess Diana hair and a brace on her teeth. She always covered her mouth when she giggled and said 'Yah' instead of yes. But Maggie was different. She stood with her hands on her big hips, looking me up and down, smirking. She looked much older than sixteen. She'd recently had her hair cut into a very short, butch style which made her look even tougher.

She wasn't the usual sort of Lady Margaret Lancaster pupil. She was a scholarship girl too, but that was all we had in common. Apart from *being* common. But I minded desperately and attended to my accent and never talked about my home or family. A lot of the girls sneered at me in consequence. Maggie didn't give a damn about the way she talked, deliberately jettisoning aitches and inserting ain'ts. She lived on a council estate and talked about it so amusingly that all the girls who lived in mock-Tudor mansions envied her like mad. Maggie had a tough, glamorous boy-friend even when she started at the school. She was now rumoured to be so sexually experienced that Shere Hite could write a whole book about her. She had passed the stiff scholarship exam so she must be clever, but she mucked about so much in lessons and did her homework so rarely that she was near the bottom of the lowest stream. She had failed most of her mock O levels and hadn't seemed to mind at all. When the teachers told her off she just smiled unpleasantly. The way she was now smiling at me.

'You look as if you're about to start blubbing,' she said. 'Come on, Louise.'

She barged past me and sauntered into a classroom. We followed. Children milled about in all directions, choosing what they wanted to do. I was taken aback. There had been a makeshift Wendy House and some Lego bricks and a tattered reading corner at my primary school – but this room was how I imagined Hamley's. I gazed at the easels and the pots of paint and the stack of smooth, white paper, the flotilla of little boats and fish and jugs and teapots and watering cans bobbing in the blue water trough, the wooden indoor climbing-frame, the giant bricks, the big blobs of pink and yellow dough. If only I had the room to myself and could have a proper play!

A middle-aged woman in an ultramarine overall seemed to be doing just that. She was down on all fours, loading a long toy train with alphabet cubes, saying in a silly voice, 'Chuff chuff, I'm Tony the train, I want to be filled up with all these lovely bricks.'

A cluster of toddlers watched her warily.

'Christ,' said Maggie Turner.

Louise giggled anxiously and the woman looked up.

'Ah! Girls! How lovely,' she said brightly, getting to her feet. 'Come along darlings, fill up Tony the train.'

For one astonished second I thought she was still talking to us. It was a relief when she handed out bricks to the watching children and came over to us, beaming. She wore scarlet lipstick and buttercup yellow clogs. Working in a nursery school seemed to have given her a taste for powder-paint colours.

'Mrs Philpotts' told me all about you. I'm Mrs Adamson. And you're Katherine Petworthy, Margaret Turner and Louise Joplin. Who's who?'

We mumbled names.

'And you all want to be nursery school teachers?' she said warmly.

We shuffled.

'Actually, I really want to teach English,' said Louise.

'Really? Oh well, we must let you read at Storytime,' said Mrs Adamson, as if it was a great treat.

'And what about you, Katherine?'

I hesitated. I couldn't possibly say I wanted to be a professor, not in front of Maggie.

'I want to do senior teaching too,' I said lamely.

'What subject?'

'I'm not really sure.'

'Well, what are you best at?' Mrs Adamson said relentlessly.

Maggie and Louise exchanged glances.

I was best at everything, except games. I'd got the highest mark for English Literature and English Language, over ninety per cent in both subjects.

'English,' I mumbled.

'Well, well, another story-teller!' Her eyes swivelled to Maggie. 'Don't tell me we have yet another English specialist here?'

'No fear,' said Maggie. 'I just like little kids, that's all.'

Maggie like little kids? I could see her giving one of the little darlings a quick smack around the head if they stepped out of line. But I was wrong.

Maggie and I were in Mrs Adamson's room with her morning children. Louise got shunted off to Miss Hickson's all-day children in another class-room altogether. Maggie and Louise groaned at the idea of being separated and asked why I couldn't go to Miss Hickson.

'Now, now, even my little ones go where they're told without complaining,' said Mrs Adamson.

Maggie made vomiting noises which Mrs Adamson chose to ignore.

'This is the most important half-hour of the morning,' said Mrs Adamson, moving to another group of nose-picking toddlers and putting a large biscuit tin of beads in their midst. 'Even some of our old-timers of four feel a little insecure when they say goodbye to Mummy. We must do our best to get them occupied straight away. So help to get the children settled, girls. Now, who's going to make a lovely necklace?'

I stood watching her inadequately, but Maggie immediately walked over to two little girls fighting over a limp ballet dress from the dressing-up trunk.

'Here, steady on. You'll tear it in two, you silly little twits. Let's find you something much better. What's in this old trunk? Ooh, look at these lovely evening dresses. You have the

84

red, Curlylocks. And you have this sparkly white one. Aren't they pretty?'

A little boy with National Health glasses reached out timidly for the discarded ballet dress.

'You don't want that, do you, Sunshine? Oh I say, whatever turns you on, ducky,' said Maggie camply, and the children giggled.

I dithered from one group of children to the next, trying to look as if I was behaving constructively. Gavin was in the painting corner digging his hand into a pot of brown paint and smearing great disgusting splodges over his paper. I knew exactly what he was thinking, the dirty little beast.

'Why don't you use one of these nice paintbrushes, Gavin?' I suggested, talking in a matey Maggie voice.

Gavin ignored me. I repeated myself.

'Don't have to,' he said sulkily.

'But you'd do a much better painting if – '

'Miss! *Miss*! We're allowed to do finger-painting aren't we?' Gavin bawled.

Mrs Adamson's head bobbed out of the Wendy House window.

'That's right, dear,' she called.

'See!' said Gavin, wagging his head at me.

I left the painting corner and hung around the water trough for a while. I tried to instigate an educational pouring game, but the children were suspicious.

'Shall we play storms instead?' I said desperately. 'We'll make it start raining, shall we? All these little boats are bobbing around helplessly. One of them can be wrecked. This little red one.'

'No! That's my boat!'

'The yellow one then, I don't care. Come on, let's make torrential rain with the watering-cans.'

'I'm not sure that's a very good idea, Katherine,' said Mrs Adamson, materialising behind me. 'The children aren't really allowed to splash like that. And I can see two people without their plastic sleeves and aprons. Oh dear, Tanya, your woollie! It's sodden. You are a silly, aren't you?'

Mrs Adamson obviously thought me a silly too. I stared sullenly at Maggie, who had a whole tribe of admirers clustered round her. The little girl who had wanted to go home was standing in the doorway now, still clutching her mother. I went up to them.

The mother's face brightened a little.

'Are you helping, dear? It's lovely here, isn't it? This is my little girl, Samantha, Sammy we call her. She's a little bit shy, but she'll come round soon, I'm sure. She only started at Easter, that's why she's a bit . . ... She's better than she was though, she used to scream the whole three hours.'

I looked at Sammy in awe. She hid her damp face in her mother's stomach.

'Oh Sammy! Don't, you'll have me over. Are you going to go and play with this nice girl while I go and nip round Sainsbury's, eh?'

'Want to come too,' Sammy muttered.

'No dear, of course you don't. You want to stay in the nursery and play with all the lovely toys,' the mother lied firmly.

She tried to peel Sammy from her skirt, prizing her little fingers back.

'Now you be a good girl. You promised not to make a fuss. Don't you show me up. No more tears now.'

Tears immediately sprang from Sammy's watery blue eyes and she screwed up her face in despair. I stared at her, appalled.

'Oh dear, oh dear, what's that silly noise?' said Mrs Adamson, vaulting nimbly over the wall of bricks and landing beside us. 'Hello, Sammy! Come here, poppet. Let's see what you'd like to play with today.' She picked her up and said over her shoulder, 'I should go now, Mrs Grieve. Don't worry, she'll settle soon, you know she does now.'

Mrs Grieve scuttled off.

'Have you met Katherine, Sammy?' said Mrs Adamson, carrying her into a corner. 'If you stop that silly noise maybe Katherine will play with you for a bit. Here's the Noah's Ark. You like that, don't you, dear? Sit with her, Katherine. She'll stop crying in two shakes of a lamb's tail, just get her absorbed.'

Mrs Adamson parked her on a cushion and went dashing off. Tears dripped relentlessly down Sammy's face.

I took the lid off the Noah's Ark and started to get the animals out. I found a fat, grey sheep.

'Here. It's a lamb and it's shaking its tail. Once, twice. Now. You've got to stop crying.'

Sammy looked at me blankly and went on dripping.

'Are you going to help me line up the animals?' I said, fishing more out.

I looked longingly at the water trough. It would be marvellous to float the Ark on the water and act it out properly but I knew Mrs Adamson was unlikely to approve.

'Here's Mr Noah,' I said, scrabbling inside the Ark and finding him. 'Oh dear, poor man, I bet it was uncomfortable squashed underneath that great elephant.'

Sammy didn't smile. She cried silently, picking at the hem of her silly, skimpy shorts.

'Why don't you find Mrs Noah? She'll smooth him down and tidy his beard. He's feeling a bit ruffled. Look, there she is. That round pink lady.'

Sammy refused to co-operate, but Gavin came wandering along, brown paint right up to his elbows. He hovered, peering over my shoulder. I shuffled away from him and went on talking to the Noahs and their large menagerie.

'That's old Macdonald and his farm,' said Gavin. 'Eeh-aye eeh-aye oh. Isn't it, Miss?'

'No. It's Noah and Mrs Noah and their Ark.'

'No it ain't. It's Macdonald. Miss sings that song. What you putting them like that for?'

He squatted down and flicked at my line of neatly paired animals. They went down like ninepins.

'Stop it! They've got to go in the Ark. Leave them alone.'

'Don't want to. Look at them cows.' He sniggered, fingering their shocking-pink udders.

Sammy went on weeping, but a smirk briefly puckered her mouth.

'Leave them alone. They want to go into the Ark.'

'Ark?'

'This! Don't you know the story?'

'Why do they want to go in that boat thing?'

'Because it's going to rain and there's going to be a flood. It's in the Bible. God sends a terrible flood because everyone's been so wicked but he saves Noah and all the animals.'

'What's a flood?'

'You know what a flood is. After it's been raining and raining.'

'But it's not raining,' said Gavin, and he sighed heavily and screwed his filthy forefinger into his head to indicate the extent of my madness.

I remembered Wendy.

'You think I'm mad, don't you? Well, I am mad. Only when there's a full moon though. I keep myself under control the rest of the time.' I went through the whole bit, but it sounded silly and self-conscious. Gavin and Sammy were neither frightened nor impressed. They started flicking all the animals over, giggling stupidly.

'Katherine!' Mrs Adamson was standing behind me, looking dubious. 'A word in your ear, dear.'

She smiled at me very brightly indeed, lipstick smears dimming the gleaming enamel. 'I think we'd better be a little careful about imaginary games. Nothing too odd and morbid. Now, as Gavin and Sammy are playing nicely together, why don't you go and help Maggie dress the children up. They *do* look as if they're having fun.'

Everyone had fun that day but me. Mrs Adamson clearly didn't trust me on my own with the children. She made me tag on to Maggie Turner or else do menial tasks like handing round the milk bottles or measuring out paint. I even had to clear up a puddle in the corner of the lavatories.

She did ask me to perform when it was story time, but when I asked if I could make up my own story she beamed her teeth at me again and said she thought the children might prefer a few old favourites out of books. So I read *Topsy and Tim* and the Ladybird *Little Red Hen* and an uninspiring *Mr Man*. I read with great expression and the children listened politely enough, but did not seem over enthusiastic. They sat in a semicircle with Mrs Adamson and Maggie. There was great competition to sit next to Maggie.

When it was time for the morning children to go home, nearly all of them said special goodbyes to her. The only child who bothered to say goodbye to me was Gavin. He tugged at the back of my skirt and said, 'Cheerio, Miss.' I warmed to him a little until I discovered he'd left a thick smear of brown paint on the back of my school skirt. It made me look as if I'd had a horrible accident.

I had to sit with Maggie and Louise while we ate a nursery lunch of fish fingers and spaghetti and jam sponge pudding and custard. They talked to each other. Every so often they whispered and shrieked with laughter and looked at me.

I tried again with the afternoon children, hoping there might just be *one* who was funny and odd and different, but I had a similar lack of success. I have never been so glad for it to be five o'clock in all my life. The moment Mrs Adamson said we could go I ran out of the squat little building – and there at the gate stood Richard, waiting for me.

Chapter 9

'Richard!'

He was wearing his soft checked shirt and his cords and his hair fell over his forehead and he had a big smile on his face. His arm went round my waist, hugging me.

'Well? Was it as bad as you thought?'

'Worse! Much worse. Oh Richard, it's so lovely to see you. Why aren't you at work?'

'I have been. I nipped out a few minutes early and charged down to the school. Do you have to go straight home or shall we go for a little walk?'

'We'll go for a walk,' I said at once, although I knew Dad would be expecting me back right that minute.

I heard familiar giggles behind me. Louise, and Maggie Turner. I held on tightly to Richard. They went on past us, both of them having a good look at Richard. He didn't seem to mind.

'Friends of yours?'

'Bitter enemies, more like. Especially Maggie, the big one.'

'She looks like Desperate Dan with that hair and those shoulders,' said Richard.

'Do you really think so?' I said delightedly. 'Most boys seem to think she's really sexy.'

'You're joking.'

'What about the other one, Louise? She's quite pretty, isn't she?'

'I suppose so. But she looks a bit boring. There are hundreds of girls just like her.'

'You're very clever about saying the right thing,' I said.

His fair hair shone in the sunlight. I could see the gold down on his skin. His shirt sleeves were rolled up and the hair on his arms was gold too. I hadn't noticed his arms before. They looked so strong, the whole geography of his arms so different from my own, but there was a surprising delicacy about the blue veins at his wrists and his graceful, pointed elbows.

I looked at our reflection in a shop window, wanting to see what we looked like together, but my own appearance depressed me.

'I look such an idiot in my school uniform. Are you sure you don't mind being seen with me?' I asked, semi-seriously.

'I'm *proud* to be seen with you.'

'Really? I thought you'd gone off me on Sunday.'

'What on earth gave you that idea?'

'I was so silly about giving my ice-cream to that old lady.'

'I didn't mind. I thought it was lovely of you.'

'It wasn't. It was just – well, I know I'll end up like that, lonely and pathetic and my coat falling to bits.'

'No you won't! You'll be a very happy cosseted old lady and I tell you what, I'll buy you a brand new fur coat every year for your birthday.'

My heart started thudding, but I knew it was just a joke, of course, a pretend game very much to my taste.

'Not fur, I don't think; I don't really fancy covering myself with all those little corpses. I'd keep imagining their glazed eyes and their scrabbly paws. No, I rather fancy shawls, great thick, cashmere shawls, the sort that are always mentioned in Victorian novels.'

'Right, a new shawl then, a different colour every year.'

'And a new dress too? I'm going to be a gaudy old lady, I don't want soft greys and pastels, and I'm never going to wear black either. I want lovely, brilliant, flowery dresses, rich Paisleys, vibrant checks and stripes, and I'll have coloured stockings to match, to hide my varicose veins.'

'Lovely,' said Richard, blinking.

'What about you? What shall I buy you on your birthdays?'

'I won't need anything. Just so long as I've got you.'

'Oh Richard. You must want something.'

'How about a kiss?'

He pulled me behind a bus shelter and kissed me there in the street in broad daylight.

'And me in my Lady Margaret Lancaster uniform. I shall get expelled.'

'You don't sound very concerned.'

'It would be wonderful. Then it wouldn't matter about my O levels. No, I'm not going to think about them, why did I have to say that? To hell with my O levels. You won't mind if I don't get A grades, will you, Richard?'

'Not a bit.'

'You won't mind if I fail them altogether?'

'You can get Z grades in them all, for all I care.'

'You are a pal, Richard.'

'I'm more than that, aren't I?'

'More than what?'

'I'm not just a friend?'

'You can be my best friend if you want,' I said shyly. 'I've never had a best friend.'

I'd always longed for a special friend with whom I could share everything. A friend that I wouldn't have to pretend to. A friend who liked me just for myself. I had Nicola, but sisters didn't really count. Besides, half the time she annoyed me so.

'I've had heaps of best friends,' said Richard. 'But you're more than that. Come down here a minute. I don't feel like making declarations in the middle of a main road.'

He led me down a side-street. Half of the houses were derelict, with blind brick windows and corrugated iron doors. Weeds waved triumphantly, the little lawns and rosebushes long overwhelmed.

Richard pulled me into one of the gardens. We waded through couch-grass and dodged nettles until we got to the house itself.

'Let's go round the back. Come on,' said Richard, trampling down brambles for me.

'Is this where you take all your girls?' I said, starting to giggle. 'It's so romantic, all this lush nature running rampant, and the enchanting odour of rotting vegetation and cats. My pulse is throbbing expectantly.'

'Don't, Katy,' said Richard. He stood still. 'Where would you like to go then? There's not really time to go to the park, is there?'

I realised I'd hurt him.

'Oh Richard, I was just joking. I *like* it here. Don't sulk.'

'I'm not sulking. It's just I wanted to find somewhere special and private and lovely and I end up dragging you to this old dump.'

He hit out at the wall of the house, a little harder than he'd meant to. I saw him wince and picked up his hand.

'You've grazed the knuckle, you idiot.'

'It's all right. It doesn't hurt.'

He tried to pull his hand away but I held on to it.

'Richard?'

He put both arms round me and pulled me close to kiss me.

My eyes closed automatically but after a minute I opened them, and there were Richard's brown eyes an inch away from me, making me jump a little and stop kissing and laugh.

'You're meant to close your eyes. It's more romantic.'

'I'd sooner look at you.' He hesitated, and then said softly, 'I love you.'

I felt my arms prickle and I shivered.

'I love you too,' I mumbled, embarrassed.

There was a little pause.

'Feel my pulse. It really *is* throbbing,' I said.

Richard burst out laughing and gave me a big hug.

'Oh I do love you. I've been wanting to say that to you and it's been so difficult and yet now it's so easy. I love you, I love you, I love you.'

'I love you. The words aren't enough. I really do love you, Richard. Funny, I've never really believed in love.'

'But you do now?'

'Implicitly.'

'Don't use long words. I'm thick, remember?'

'Don't you dare call yourself thick.'

'I am compared to you.'

'That's rubbish. And I'm not clever anyway, not any more. I'm not even sure I ever was. I just worked like mad, harder than any of the others. I've kept everyone fooled up till now, even myself. But it's been a struggle ever since I started the O level syllabus, because it hasn't been just learning, it's been working things out, and it's got harder and harder, and then when I took the actual O levels my brain just exploded from overwork.'

'Yes, what's this grey tentacle oozing out of your ear? Dead brain?' He pretended to pluck it out.

'I wish you really could pull it all out, all the memory and the worry parts.'

I saw the time on his watch.

'I'll have to go in a minute. I'm ever so late.'

'You're like Cinderella.'

'These are hardly glass slippers,' I said, kicking out one leg and displaying my hideous Clarks school sandals.

'Well, I'm not your actual Prince Charming, am I?' said Richard.

'Yes, you are. To me you are,' I said, and then blushed because it sounded so wet. But it seemed to please Richard enormously.

'Then I've got to waken you with a kiss, haven't I?'

'Hang on, we've swopped fairy-tales. Never mind.'

'Let's keep swopping. I'll put on my frog disguise, and then I get to come and sleep in your bed,' said Richard.

I smiled but then he gave that awful leering wink and spoilt it all. I felt hot with sudden irritation. Richard tried to kiss me again but I turned my head away quickly.

'What's up?' he said anxiously.

'I want to stay here,' I said. 'I don't ever want to go back home. I hate it. I hate them.' It was safer to be angry with them.

'No you don't.'

'I do.'

'You don't hate your mum.'

'I hate her more than anyone,' I said, surprising myself. 'And I hate my father and my sister.'

No, I didn't hate Nicola, and yet just recently her love had been so cloying that I'd wanted to keep pushing her away, and now I seemed to have pushed too hard. We still hadn't made friends properly, although we kept up appearances in front of Mum and Dad. I wondered if she'd gone to school today. I could still scarcely believe that timid old Nicola had dared play truant all this time. I ought to do something about it, make her go to school, maybe even tell Mum and Dad. No, Dad would half kill her.

I shook my head irritably. 'I don't want to think about them. I wish they didn't even exist. I'd like a great hurricane to come whirling down Waverton Avenue and whisk up the shop with Mum and Dad and Nicola neatly tucked away inside.'

94

'And where would they end up? Munchkin land?' Richard suddenly squatted and did a funny little dance. 'Follow, follow, follow, follow, follow the yellow brick road,' he sang, in a fat Munchkin voice. 'Dance with me, Dorothy,' he demanded, his arms round my knees.

I shook him off gently.

'I'm not Dorothy. I'm more like the Wicked Witch. Get *up*, Richard. I wish I was a witch. I could put a spell on everyone then. Turn all those vile little nursery kids into waxworks and then light a great big fire in the Wendy House and watch them melt. Drip, drip, little snub noses trickle away, tiny fingers fall off one at a time – '

'Katy! You haven't half got a sinister imagination.'

'Mrs Adamson thinks so too,' I said, sighing.

I told him all about my day at the nursery school, exaggerating a little to make it more interesting. I had him in fits of laughter.

'You're making it all up.'

'I swear I'm not.'

'But you were such a success with Wendy.'

'What?'

'My sister. She thought you were smashing.'

'She didn't.'

'She did. She's been going on about you ever since. She's got the whole family intrigued. You'll have to come to tea to set their curiosity at rest.'

'I didn't think she liked me at all.'

'You keep putting yourself down. I bet all the little kids at the nursery have gone rushing home to tell their mums about this lovely, weird Katy who plays with them all day.'

'No, it was Maggie they liked, not me.'

'Then they've got no taste at all. Old Desperate Dan?'

'Go on calling her that. Here, let's see your watch again. Oh goodness. I've got to go.'

'I'll walk back with you. Katy, can I come and say hello to your mother again?'

'The shop will be shut.'

'Can't you invite me in?'

'Oh Richard. Look, if you don't believe me about my Dad, ask Mark, ask anyone. If he knew I was seeing you he'd go mad. I've never even taken a *girl* friend home.'

I tried to explain all the way home. When we got to the top of Waverton Parade I saw Dad waiting on the shop doorstep, his arms folded. I couldn't see the expression on his face at that distance, but I didn't need to. I gabbled a goodbye to Richard and ran towards the row.

'Where the hell have you been, Madam? What's going on? What sort of a school is this, keeping you out till all hours? What have you been up to?' Dad exploded, when I was still only half-way down the street.

Richard came to meet me from the nursery school every evening that week but he didn't try to persuade me to confide in Dad again. He'd seen for himself that it would be impossible.

He did keep trying to tell me that I was exaggerating my failure at the nursery – but Gavin and Sammy and Co refused to take me to their tiny hearts. Maggie and Louise weren't quite so horrible though. They asked me all about Richard, and although not exactly impressed, they thawed considerably. I wasn't such an odd, swotty brainbox after all. I was half-way human. I had a boy-friend.

Mrs Adamson kept me safely occupied with menial tasks for the rest of the week. After several days she forgot to be tactful about it.

'Oh dear, there seems to be a little fracas in the Wendy House. What's all that silly squabbling? Kenneth, put that iron *down*, darling. I think Julie had it first. Anyway, you mustn't hit her with it. Maggie, leave that tidying and go and sort them out, will you? Katherine, you don't mind finishing tidying the dressing-up box for Maggie, do you, dear? Maggie does seem to have more of a knack with the children, doesn't she?'

I agreed through gritted teeth. I tidied the dressing-up clothes and came across an old pair of white high-heeled shoes. I tried one on surreptitiously. It was half a size too small, but not unbearably tight. The shoes didn't really belong to anyone. They were certainly wasted on a lot of silly toddlers. I smuggled them out wrapped in my old cardigan.

My week's Work Experience had taught me nothing at all, but I had gained a decent pair of heeled shoes at long last.

Chapter 10

I wore the stolen shoes on Saturday. I told them at home that Mrs Adamson had invited Maggie and Louise and me to tea because she was so pleased with us.

'I should think so too,' Dad grumbled. 'She's been getting free labour from you lot, hasn't she? Damn daft idea this Work Experience scheme. If you want a bit of work experience then why can't you help me out in the shop? What's the use of sending you to a nursery school? They're a waste of bally time in themselves. Mothers should stay at home with their kiddies, not go gallivanting off to work . . .'

I was happy to let him rant, just so long as he believed I was going to be with Mrs Adamson on Saturday. Mum grew agitated, worried that I might wear my jeans and shame her. She was relieved when I told her I'd wear my blue flowery dress.

'But I'll need tights, Mum,' I said artfully.

'Can't you make do with your long white socks? The skirt's long on that dress. They won't really show much,' Mum said.

'I can't wear socks,' I said firmly. 'Besides they're not white any more. They're all that awful grey colour. I can't wear them, Mum, they don't look *clean.*'

That worried her so much that she gave me fifty pence out of her housekeeping for tights. I used fifteen pence of my pocket-money so that I could afford nice Mary Quant tights, pretty white ones.

'What a waste. What did you get white for? You might just as well have worn your socks,' said Mum crossly. 'And I thought you'd bring me back some change. They've got decent flesh-coloured tights in Woolies for only 39p.'

I took no notice. The daisy motif on the tights packet had given me an idea. I closeted myself in my bedroom with the

97

clothes I was really going to wear, an old denim skirt and my school blouse. The denim skirt was two years old and too small for me, but I'd seen several girls wearing really short skirts recently, so I thought it wouldn't look too bad. I got white and yellow thread and embroidered lazy daisies all round the short hem to liven it up a bit, and then I stitched more daisies on the collar and cuffs of my blouse. I could always unpick them before school started again.

I tried them on with my new tights and the white high-heels. I wasn't sure, but I thought the outfit worked. It looked a bit shabby and home-made, but in an odd, interesting, art-studenty sort of way. Nicola came barging into the bedroom as I was preening in front of the mirror.

'Where did you get the shoes from?' she gasped.

'Sh! Louise gave them to me.'

'You lucky thing! Let me try them on, eh?'

'Your feet are much wider than mine, you know they are. You'll stretch them.'

'All right, selfish. You do look grown-up. But Dad will never let you go out like that, you know he won't.'

'He won't notice,' I said firmly, brushing my hair. Brushing and brushing, but in vain. 'It looks even worse after I've done it. I think I'll shave it all off,' I said in despair, flinging my hairbrush down.

'I love those daisies. Will you do them on my skirt too? Yours is ever so short now. It looks a bit – you know. Of *course* he'll notice, he'll hear you going out and call you in to say goodbye, you know he will.'

'So I'll be wearing this, won't I?' I said, getting my appalling flowery frock out of the wardrobe and pulling it over my head. It was so voluminous it covered my blouse and skirt easily. I put my white shoes in an old carrier and stuck my feet into my awful school sandals.

'I *see*,' said Nicola. 'Will you change at Mrs Adamson's then?'

'I'll change in the ladies' lav in Partridge Street,' I said, turning my back on my hideous image in the mirror.

'Are you really going to Mrs Adamson's?' Nicola asked, sitting on the end of her bed and stroking Sniffle.

'Where else would I be going?'

'You're not going there, are you? You're seeing *him!*'

'So what?' I said, as coolly as possible.

'So you aren't half going to catch it if you're found out,' said Nicola, turning Sniffle over and tickling his matted tummy. She reached out for my hairbrush and started brushing him tenderly.

'Nicola, that's my hairbrush. Give it here!'

'I'm only grooming him.'

'Yes, well I don't want my hairbrush round that filthy old flea-bitten animal.'

'Katherine! How could you? You've hurt his feelings terribly. Look at his ears drooping.'

'Don't be so stupid. How can you be so babyish, always twittering on about toy animals at your age,' I snapped, snatching back my hairbrush – but I found it hard to meet Sniffle's baleful blue eyes. I knew he wasn't real, of course, but I had once passionately believed that he was a proper person.

'He's crying now, look. Big tears,' said Nicola reproachfully, rocking Sniffle in her arms.

'Stop sniffling, Sniffle,' I said sternly.

Nicola's face brightened.

'Where are you going with this Richard?' she asked.

'Stop calling him "this" Richard. I'm not sure. I think we might be going to the pictures,' I said, knowing poor Nicola would be envious.

We went to the cinema so seldom that every trip was a magical event. Dad had taken us to our first film as a Christmas treat. It was *The Tales of Beatrix Potter*. We hadn't read the books but Dad knew it was ballet and therefore cultural, even though it was a children's film. He got bored very quickly and nodded off, but Nicola and I were enraptured. For months afterwards we teetered on the toes of our bedroom slippers doing the Pigling Bland and Pigwig pas de deux and leapt about like loonies being Jeremy Fisher until Nicola slipped on the hearthrug that she was using as a waterlily pad and sprained her ankle.

Dad told us both off for being such fools, but every Christmas holiday he still took us to a film. We saw *Swallows and Amazons* and *The Railway Children* and *Chitty Chitty Bang Bang* but for the last few years we had missed out. Dad said there

99

weren't any films fit for children nowadays. It was all Filth on at the Kinema, and he wasn't going to pollute our brains with Muck.

'What are you going to see?' Nicola said, looking agonised.

'I don't know what's on.'

'You're so *lucky*.'

'I hope it's Muck and Filth,' I said.

Nicola giggled. 'It's bound to be. The cinema's a disgrace nowadays,' she said, trying to imitate Dad. She paused. 'Here, Katherine, what are you up to nowadays? Is this Richard your boy-friend? Speak up, young lady. Spit it out.' She was still doing her Dad imitation, but the question was obviously serious.

'Stop calling him this. How many times do I have to tell you? Yes, he's my boy-friend. What of it?' I said belligerently, but I could feel my face going hot.

Nicola shrugged, laying Sniffle down on the bed.

'It just seems so funny, that's all. You having a boy-friend. I didn't think you even liked boys.'

'I don't. Most of them.'

'But you like this . . . you like Richard?'

'Yes.'

'Do you *love* him?'

'Nicola! Honestly,' I said, checking everything in my carrier. 'I've got to go, I'm late.'

'I wish you didn't have Richard. It's horrible without you,' said Nicola.

I stared at her, stricken.

'Don't be silly,' I said automatically. 'Look Nic, you've got to learn to get along without me sometimes. Can't you make some friends of your own? What about some of the girls at school?'

She gave me the look I deserved.

'There must be *someone* nice there,' I persisted.

'They're all hateful.'

'Are you still playing truant?'

'No,' Nicola said hurriedly, but when I made her look at me she nodded.

'You are an idiot. Look, you've *got* to go.'

'It's so awful.'

100

'It's going to get worse the more you stay away. Have you been messing around all this week?'

'I went on Monday, honestly. Only all these girls ganged up on me in the lavatories and kept pulling my hair and one of them had some manicure scissors and she kept pretending to be cutting my hair with them. I *can't* go, Kath. You don't know what they're like.'

'They're only teasing. If you'd just laugh at them, try to join in the joke, then they'd stop being so horrible.'

'No they wouldn't.'

'Well, stand up for yourself. Tell them you'll smash their teeth in if they won't leave you alone. I bet you just stand there and pull faces and cry.'

'Yes,' Nicola agreed miserably.

'Then you *deserve* to be treated like that. Oh Nic, you've got to try.'

'I don't want to try.'

'You want friends, don't you?'

'No. Not that lot. You're my friend.'

'But I'm your sister.'

'That doesn't make any difference. You can still be my best friend, can't you?'

'Yes, I suppose so. But I want other friends too.'

'You didn't. Not till this Richard.'

'Stop saying *this*! I've got to go, I'm meeting him at half past.'

I abandoned her and crept down the stairs, but Dad heard me even above the sound of 'Grandstand' and called me in to him.

His eyes wrinkled suspiciously as he stared at me. I tried to look unconcerned, but I was sweating inside my school blouse. He couldn't see through my dress, could he?

'What's in the carrier bag?'

I jumped. 'Just. . . .' Oh God, *what?* 'Slippers! Mrs Adamson asked us to bring them. They've got new, pale carpets.'

'What a cheek! Who does she think she is? And what are you going there for, anyway? I didn't think you thought much of her. You were going on about her as if you couldn't stand her.'

'She's all right. When you get to know her.'

'I can see the point of you being all pally with Miss Hyde, I mean she's your proper teacher, but this nursery school lady, you're just wasting your time, Katherine. Why do you *want* to have tea with her? And what time are you going to be back, for Heaven's sake?'

'Probably not till quite late, Dad. She – she's got this card game she thought we'd like to play. Look, I must go, I'm meeting the others down the road.'

'Well, watch how you go. And I'd come back home straight after tea and never mind about damn daft card games. You watch the roads and walk quickly past the pubs, do you hear? Look, shall I come and meet you, might that be better? Where exactly does she live?'

'Oh Dad, don't be silly. I can walk back with the others. Dad, I'm *late*.'

'All right, all right. You've got time to give your father a kiss goodbye though, haven't you?'

I stared at him, surprised. We hardly ever kissed. I shuffled towards his armchair and awkwardly bent over. Our cheeks touched briefly as we both kissed air.

'You're growing up too fast,' Dad muttered. 'You're not my little girl any more.'

'Oh *Dad*.'

What would he say if he saw me in my skirt and shoes! It was an enormous relief to get out of the house at last. I was used to Nicola twining round me like ivy, but it was so weird for Dad to start too.

I still had the feel of his dry, whiskery cheek on mine. I brushed my face with my hand and started running. By the time I'd done a detour into the Ladies and stuffed my floral frock and school shoes in my carrier I was hopelessly late for Richard.

He was standing outside the Odeon, shifting from one foot to the other, whistling under his breath. He was wearing the cream jacket again. He didn't look right. And he didn't sound right either.

'Hi, sweetheart,' he said, as I hurried uncertainly up to him, not used to my high heels.

It sounded so false and silly that I scowled.

'What's up?'

'Nothing.'

'Well, why's your face tripping you?'

102

That was another expression I couldn't stand.

'I'm fine, really. I'm sorry I'm late. My Dad went on and on.'

'Oh well. Give us a kiss, eh?'

I stiffened. There were crowds of people outside the cinema. It just wasn't an appropriate place. Couldn't he see that for himself?

'Not here,' I mumbled.

'Oh – huffy. Okay, suit yourself.'

I felt like hitting him. What was the *matter* with him? Or was it me? Why didn't he say he liked my daisy clothes, my stylish shoes? Didn't I look right after all?

We stood as stiff and silent as statues. I didn't love him, I didn't even *like* him.

'Are we going to the pictures then?'

I nodded.

'Which film do you want to see? They say that science fiction thing's quite good. Very creepy.'

I had read all the appropriate reviews in the local paper that morning, and particularly fancied a new American film about teenagers. But I smiled wanly and agreed on the science fiction film even though the reviews had said it was rubbish.

'Unless you'd rather see one of the other films,' said Richard.

I hesitated. 'Well, I read this review – but it doesn't matter.'

We had a silly five minute argument which ended in Richard insisting on buying two tickets for the American teenage film. I followed him guiltily up the steps, wobbling dangerously in my high heels. My little toes were terribly pinched and I had blisters starting on both heels, but I was prepared to suffer for my looks.

I stumbled in the dark cinema. Richard's hand was immediately on my arm, supporting me.

'Careful,' he whispered, cuddling me into him. The itch of my irritation eased a little. He smelt pleasantly but inappropriately of floral scented talcum powder. I liked the idea of him borrowing it from his mother so that he wouldn't get too hot and sweaty with me. I imagined him pink and damp after a bath, annointing his armpits with powder, and I smiled in the darkness.

We sat down at the end of a row and stared obediently at the

103

screen. We sat through ten minutes of a dull travelogue about Scotland. Richard fidgeted rather a lot. I felt guiltier and hoped the main film would prove worth watching.

The lights went up at the end of the Scottish film and Richard stretched.

'That seemed to go on for ever.'

'I'm sorry.'

'It's not your fault.' Richard peered along the row of seats. 'I'm just checking on old ladies before I offer you an ice-cream.'

I smiled, falling in love with him all over again. I wondered if I dared ask him not to borrow his brother's horrible jacket. It didn't fit at the shoulders and pulled badly at the back, making his bottom stick out. I was trying to work up the courage while he went to queue for two choc ices but as soon as he got back we were both diverted.

'Rick! I *thought* it was you. What you doing here then, mate?'

A boy in the row behind stuck his head between us, grinning delightedly. He had an almost identical cream jacket but he wore it with style. His hair fanned out in a long dark quiff. He jerked his head every few seconds to clear his forehead of hair. He was good looking in a greasy sort of way, the sort of boy Richard seemed to want to try to be, the sort of boy I couldn't bear.

'Hello, Terry,' said Richard, and to my dismay he sounded enthusiastic.

'This your girl then, Rick?' said Terry, nodding his head at me.

Rick. I couldn't bear it. I was suddenly very much my father's daughter. How could he turn a good, sturdy name like Richard into such an appalling nickname? And I never in a million years wanted to be known as Rick's Girl. But I had to smile and nod sociably as Richard introduced me.

'This is my girl, Jeanette,' said Terry, putting his arm round the girl sitting next to him.

Jeanette said 'hello' brightly. She was pretty. Very, very pretty. She had long, fair hair that fell in soft waves almost to her waist, real fairy princess hair, and one of those cute, pert little faces, all big eyes, snub nose and perky smile. She was wearing marvellous clothes, a white lace blouse and a tight,

104

green, velvet jacket with huge sleeves. Oh God, no wonder Richard had kept tactfully quiet about my clothes. How could I ever have thought I looked all right in a blouse that was still obviously school uniform, a child's denim skirt and a pair of jumble shoes. And my hair – I could *feel* it bristling, thousands of frizzy little ends flying in mid air. I wanted to hide under my seat, not conduct a conversation with Jeanette and Terry.

Not that I was contributing more than a few mumbled monosyllables. Terry and Richard were busy catching up on each other's news. They had apparently been in the same form at school. Terry now worked in a jeans boutique. Jeanette worked there too. I imagined the agony of the inadequate little changing room, Jeanette peering round the curtain, raising her eyebrows at my awful knickers, sneering as the new jeans sagged sadly on my childish figure . . . .

It was an enormous relief when the lights dimmed again. There were a great many adverts and previews. We could hear Terry and Jeannette whispering and giggling behind us. I wanted Richard and me to seem equally compatible but I couldn't think of anything at all to say, and he seemed to be similarly struck dumb. And then the main film started – and I watched the screen with my mouth open, growing hotter and hotter.

It was the first AA film I had ever seen. It was very different from *The Railway Children*. It was Muck and Filth all right – astonishingly so. I had had no idea that ordinary films could be so *rude*. Barely ten minutes into the film the American girl and boy were stripping off their clothes, lying on a rug, and DOING IT. Odd little pulses started ticking all over my body. I felt so strange, sitting in this big room with Richard and fifty or sixty strangers, watching two people making love.

I jumped when Richard reached out and took hold of my hand. I was ashamed of my damp palm. I wondered if he was as affected by the film as me. He had had other girl-friends before me. I wondered if he had actually done these sort of things with them. It was harder than ever to think of Mum and Dad indulging.

Richard's hand stroked mine rhythmically. I let my own hand lie limp, embarrassed about responding. Richard's hand became more insistent. Then he leant forward and started kissing me. I had been huddled sideways in my seat to see round the man in front of me so he caught me with my head at a very awkward angle. I heard Terry and Jeannette giggle and I went rigid. Oh God, how could he do it in front of them? What would they think of us? Richard's hand stopped stroking my sticky palm and sidled upwards. It stayed several inches short of my pathetic breasts, resting uncertainly on my prominent rib cage, but it worried me a lot. The hand twitched and then moved again but I decided I'd had enough and flicked it fiercely as if it was a great pink spider. The hand retreated rapidly. Richard stopped kissing me and sat still. Our heads were still uncomfortably at angles. I heard Terry whisper something and Jeanette exploded into further giggles. I extracted my head from Richard's arm and hunched miserably in my seat, trying to concentrate on the film.

The teenage lovers had finished their own love-making more satisfactorily. They were lying back limply on the hearth-rug. She covered herself with a convenient shawl, tucking it decorously under her armpits. He couldn't find a shawl for himself and there wasn't room under hers, so he just lay there brazenly, but the camera kept well above his navel. I couldn't help being disappointed. I longed to know what it actually looked like. I'd only ever seen glimpses of very little boys and classical statues, and they weren't really very informative.

I'd read about Freud and penis envy incredulously. I was exceptionally glad that I didn't have such unruly equipment hanging untidily from my own body. I gave Richard another furtive glance. It seemed so strange to think that it was there, lurking beneath his best grey trousers. I blushed in the dark and returned to the film.

They made love so many times that I began to lose count. I had no idea people did it so often. They took ridiculous risks too, until inevitably the girl's parents came home early and discovered them in the living-room sprawling naked on the white fur rug. I was amazed by the parents' reaction. They didn't even really tell her off, let alone punish her. They said they were sad that she'd felt the need to deceive them, but they didn't really seem to *mind* that she had been making love with a boy. She was fifteen, the same age as me.

I tried to imagine Dad coming into the living-room and

106

finding Richard and me cavorting naked on the imitation sheepskin and grinned wryly.

In spite of everything I became terribly caught up in the film, living it with them, forgetting all about Richard and Terry and Jeanette, but I was jarred back to reality when the credits appeared on the screen and the lights went up. I'd spilt some of my choc ice and had chocolate stains all down my blouse, making me look more of a baby than ever. I rubbed at the stains ineffectually and then folded my arms across my front.

I arranged my face into a smile to say goodbye to Terry and Jeanette – but to my horror Terry had his arm round Richard.

'Come on, pal. We'll all go for a drink, eh?'

Richard looked at me.

'Is that all right?'

'Well, I – I've got to get back quite soon,' I said desperately.

'What's she on about?' said Terry, pulling a stupid face to express his incomprehension. 'It's only half past seven!'

'She's got a very difficult father,' said Richard, sounding embarrassed. 'But you don't have to get back quite this early, do you, Katy? It's all right if we go for just one drink, isn't it?'

It wasn't all right at all, but I nodded helplessly and followed them out of the cinema.

Chapter 11

'Are you sure you don't mind?' Richard said, as we went into the pub on the corner.

I minded badly but I smiled and told him it was fine. The pub was already crowded, but Terry pushed his way through to the back and found us a table. Wet beer mug stains ringed the formica top, as if a child had been playing with a compass. The 'Space Invaders' machine next to me pinged persistently, and a fruit machine rumbled across the way. The juke-box contributed enthusiastically to the noise. I felt my ear-drums cringing.

'Great atmosphere here, isn't it?' Terry shouted.

I smiled wanly and leant back against the red flock wall-paper.

'What you drinking then?'

I asked for a fruit juice.

'Come on, don't let's mess about with fruit juices,' said Terry impatiently. 'Have a proper drink.'

'I'd honestly just like a fruit juice,' I said, growing hot.

'Don't you like drinking?' said Jeanette.

'Have a Campari and soda, like Jeanette,' said Terry.

'I really don't want one,' I said, looking desperately at Richard.

He was sorting out change for the fruit machine, seemingly too absorbed to come to my rescue.

'I know what you'd like,' said Jeanette. 'Do you like chocolate mints?'

'Well – yes,' I said, surprised.

'Get her that chocolate mint liqueur then, Terry, she'd love that,' said Jeanette. She nodded at me maternally, although she could only be two years older than me at the most. 'Don't worry, you'll really like this liqueur, it slips down a treat. My cousin's always funny about drink and yet she loves this, she can knock back three or four no bother. What did you say your name was? Oh yeah, Katy. How long have you been going with Rick?'

'Not long.'

'Where do you work then?'

'I'm still at school.'

'Where, Malford? My little sister goes there.'

'No, it's not near here, my school,' I hedged.

'Well, which is it then?'

I was stuck.

'Lady Margaret Lancaster's.' I hoped she'd never heard of it.

'Ooh, posh! Did you hear that?' she shouted to Terry, who was standing at the bar. 'Katy goes to that public school, Lady Margaret Lancaster's, you know, with the funny uniform.'

Terry put his finger to his nose and tilted it upwards in a crude gesture. I felt blood flooding my face.

'I've always wondered what it's like at that sort of school. Is it like all them Enid Blyton stories, St Claires and Malory Towers and all those? Do you have a Mamselle and play lacrosse and have prefects?' Jeanette asked, giggling. 'What fun!'

I wasn't sure if she was sending me up or not.

'I hate it there,' I mumbled.

'Here Katy, come and try your luck,' said Richard, offering me some change.

But even that was an embarrassment, because I'd never worked a machine before and didn't have a clue what you did.

'Where you been all your life?' said Terry, as Richard patiently explained about bells and lemons and cherries. 'Has she just stepped off another planet or what, Rick?'

'She's got a mind above things like fruit machines,' said Richard. 'Katy's ever so clever. She got a scholarship to her school.'

'Oh Gawd. A brainbox as well,' said Terry. 'Here you are then, darling. One lovely mint liqueur. Wet your tonsils with that, and then tell us all about Einstein's theory of relativity and all that jazz.'

Terry and Jeanette weren't really meaning to get at me. I knew if I could only snap back with a quick answer then they'd warm towards me. But I was so shy and embarrassed I couldn't think of a thing to say. I sipped desperately at my liqueur. It tasted unbelievably disgusting but I pretended to enjoy it. I looked enviously at Jeanette's Campari. It was such a pretty colour. I should have tried one of those. Richard was drinking beer. He smiled at me but seemed almost as uneasy as I was. He must be embarrassed because I was making such a fool of myself. He was obviously wishing he had a girl-friend like Jeanette.

She started telling us a long, involved story about a very fat woman who had come into the shop to buy a pair of jeans. I could never bear funny stories about fat women, but I tittered politely when Jeanette got to the end. Terry roared with laughter, even though he'd been in the shop himself and seen it all at first hand. Richard laughed too, but he looked at me uncomfortably.

'Katy, tell Terry and Jeanette about your nursery school experience,' he said eagerly. 'It was a real laugh.'

I stared at him, appalled. Jeanette made encouraging noises. There was no way out. I stumbled through a lame account. They listened, smiling expectantly. My voice tailed into silence before anyone had enjoyed a real laugh. Jeanette and Terry looked puzzled.

'Let's have another drink,' Richard said quickly.

I asked for a Campari this time. It was another mistake. I hadn't known anything so pretty could taste so dirty.

Terry sensibly gave me up as a bad job and talked to Richard. Jeanette was left to cope with me. She told me about working in the jeans shop. She told me about this marvellous new stall in a junk market where she'd bought her beautiful, green coat. She told me about her friend's eighteenth birthday party. I made monosyllabic comments, desperately trying to think of my own topic of conversation. When Jeanette had eventually run out of things to say we sat in silence.

'I like this record,' I said at last, nodding towards the juke-box.

How could I have been so stupid? Jeanette brightened and started to discuss pop music. She kept asking me who I liked. I was horribly stuck. I didn't know anything about pop music. I heard some of the girls at school discussing their favourites, of course, but I could never join in. Dad always switched off every pop programme on the television, saying they were all raving loonies, tone deaf and obscene into the bargain. It was no use trying to listen to the radio either. Dad kept it permanently tuned to Radio Four.

I tried bluffing, but it was no use. I was eventually forced to admit my ignorance. Jeanette looked amazed and pitying, as if she'd just realised I was mentally handicapped.

'Another drink?' said Terry.

'No, I've really got to go now,' I said determinedly.

'Come on, darling, another half-hour won't hurt.'

'It will,' I said, getting up.

Richard got up too.

'Hey Rick, I thought we could all go and have a curry somewhere. I'm starving, aren't you, mate?' said Terry.

'Katy's got to get home though,' said Richard.

'You go and have a meal, Richard. I don't mind a bit,' I said quickly.

'Don't be daft. I'm coming with you,' Richard said, putting his arm round my shoulders. 'Have you got a jacket?'

'No, but – oh God!'

My carrier bag with my floral dress and my school sandals! I peered desperately under the table but I knew it couldn't be there. I'd left it in the cinema.

I waited until we'd said goodbye to Terry and Jeanette, but the minute we were outside the pub I turned to Richard.

'My carrier!' I said, and burst into tears.

It took Richard a while to understand.

'Don't worry, I'll find it for you, I promise,' he said at last.

He took my hand and we ran back to the cinema. I stood snivelling in the foyer while Richard explained to the usherette. She said nothing had been handed in, and if Richard wanted to go into the cinema he'd have to pay for another ticket. I cried harder, and the usherette called the manager, and eventually they let Richard go and look. He was a long time, but at last he emerged – clutching my carrier.

'It's all right, Katy, I've got it,' he said, but I couldn't stop crying.

He led me outside again, down a side-street until we were

111

away from all the curious stares. Then he put his arms round me and held me.

'I'm sorry,' I kept wailing.

'Don't be silly, it's not your fault,' he said, cuddling me close.

'I don't just mean my carrier,' I sobbed. 'It was so awful in the pub with your friends. I was so stupid. They thought I was pathetic and stupid and I *am*.'

'Rubbish! They liked you. You're not stupid, you're *clever*.'

'I'm hopeless. I don't know why on earth you want to see me.'

'I happen to love you. Here.' Richard fumbled in his pocket for a handkerchief. 'Your nose is running.'

'How horribly unromantic,' I said, blowing hard.

'Come on. I don't want you getting into trouble with your Dad. You'd better find somewhere to change your clothes.'

'There's a Ladies in Partridge Street. But you can't come. You mustn't see me in my terrible dress.'

'Don't be ridiculous. You're not walking home on your own.' Richard peered inside my carrier. 'It doesn't look horrible, it looks quite pretty. Come on, you silly girl.'

He walked me to the Partridge Street lavatory and waited outside while I put on the floral monstrosity and shod myself in sensible school sandals. I stayed locked inside the smelly cubicle for a good five minutes, not daring to emerge, even though it was getting later and later.

'Katy!' Richard called. 'Are you all right?'

'Of course I am,' I mumbled.

'What? Katy, come *on*. I feel so conspicuous hanging around out here. People keep looking at me as if I'm some kind of Peeping Tom. Please.'

So I walked out of the lavatory, shivering. I had hoped that it might magically have grown dark outside, but it was still light enough to see clearly. Richard looked at me.

'I told you,' I said.

'Don't be silly, it looks fine,' said Richard valiantly.

'Richard!'

'Well, it looks a bit big for you, but apart from that –'

'We'll go home by all the back streets so no one can see me.'

112

'Look, I'd be proud to be seen with you if you were wearing a black plastic dustbin liner,' said Richard.

'Why are you so *nice*?' I said, tucking my arm in his as we walked along the road. 'Be honest for a change. Wouldn't you like it if you had Jeanette for a girl-friend?'

'Jeanette? No!'

'But she's so pretty, with that lovely hair, and she can afford gorgeous clothes and she's got a really lively personality and –'

'She's all right, but she's so ordinary. No, more to the point, wouldn't you sooner have someone like Terry for a boy-friend?'

'Of course not.'

'Really?' said Richard, sounding genuinely relieved. 'He was the one who always used to get all the girls going crackers over him at school. He practically had his own fan club.'

'Well, I didn't like him. I didn't want to go off with them after the film.'

'You should have said! Were you worried about getting home in time then?'

'Not really. It'll be all right as long as I'm back by half-past nine. No, I'd have just sooner been with you. Just us.'

'Oh Katy.' He turned to me and kissed me. It was just a quick kiss at first, but then it got longer and much more passionate.

'Don't,' Richard whispered at last, shakily.

'Why?'

'Because it's so lovely and if we don't stop now I won't be able to stop at all and it's too public here and we'll get arrested for indecency,' said Richard, giving me little kisses all over my face. 'You taste salty. All those tears.'

'I am a baby.'

'You weren't acting like a baby just then.'

'Do I kiss . . . properly?'

'You kiss very improperly, which is even better.'

'I wish I didn't have to go home.'

'Don't you think I wish that too? But we're going to be able to see a lot more of each other now you're on holiday.'

'But how? I can make out I'm going to Miss Hyde's for tea again, but I can't really pretend Mrs Adamson has invited me back, they'd think that a bit odd. I was wondering about pretending to Dad that I was doing some extra studying down

113

at the reference library, but I think he knows it closes at seven, so I'd only be able to see you for a bit.'

'Never mind the evenings. We can see each other every day. Well, every afternoon at least.'

'How? You're working.'

'I've asked to go on to the night-shift for a bit. I was due to do a stint anyway. I start at half-past nine at night, finish at half-past five in the morning. I can get up at lunch-time, maybe even earlier. And we can have all afternoon together.'

'Oh Richard!'

'Pleased?'

'It's a wonderful idea. But don't you mind having to work nights?'

'Not if I can be with you during the day.'

He saw me right to the door. I said I'd try to slip out on Sunday afternoon and we kissed goodbye for a long time. It was getting very late, but when I wrenched myself away from Richard at last I stayed downstairs, thinking. It wasn't going to be that simple seeing Richard every afternoon. Dad would want me to work in the shop. Mum would want me to help with the shopping and the housework. When Nicola broke up from school she would want to trail around with me every-where. I thought of all the endless lies and evasions and arguments ahead. No. I had to find a permanent excuse.

After five minutes I ran upstairs. Mum and Nicola were absorbed in 'Dynasty' but Dad was fidgeting.

'Well, where have you been? Never mind tea, I thought you were stopping for bally breakfast at this woman's place!' he exploded. 'Come in then, don't just hover in the doorway. Tell us all about it. Speak up or has the cat got your tongue?'

'Well, I had a very nice evening,' I said lamely.

'What? Turn that row off, Nicola, I can't hear your sister properly.'

'Dynasty' flickered and vanished. Mum and Nicola looked at me reproachfully.

'There's not all that much to tell. Mrs Adamson was very nice and – '

'Very nice? What sort of a wishy-washy statement is that? You had a very nice evening. Mrs Adamson was very nice. I dare say the tea was very nice too. Very nice, Katherine, but

114

not very informative. I thought your speciality was English, eh?'

'Dad, I can't go over every single thing we said, sentence by sentence. A lot of the time Maggie and Louise and I just chatted together or played cards. Then after tea Mrs Adamson started talking to us about nursery education. She was really interesting, especially when she got on to child psychology,' I said, trying to sound convincing. Nicola wasn't helping. She was sitting with an irritating smirk on her face, making it obvious that she knew I was telling lie after lie. I prayed Dad wouldn't be distracted and look in her direction. Mum still stared at the blank television. Perhaps she was busy imagining 'Dynasty' for herself.

'You couldn't say a good word for this Mrs Adamson before,' said Dad. 'How come you've suddenly changed your opinion?'

'I suppose it's because I got to know her better tonight. We started talking about the theory of nursery school education, you see, and I began to see what all that finger-painting and pastry making is about.'

'It's about sweet B all, if you ask me,' said Dad. 'Waste of time and money, letting silly little kids mess about with muck. They'd be far better off at home with their mothers, and when they get sent to school they ought to learn their alphabet and their tables, with no fiddling about. No wonder we're becoming a nation of illiterate layabouts. If you ask me – '

'Well, I'm really interested in it all, Dad,' I said quickly, knowing I had to interrupt him and get to my point, or he'd be standing on his soap-box for hours.

'Don't tell me you want to be a nursery school teacher now!' Dad said.

'No, of course I don't – but I would like to learn more about it. Actually, Mrs Adamson asked if I'd like to carry on at the nursery school during the holidays – just in the afternoons – and I rather like the idea.'

'*What*?' Dad was predictably outraged.

I strained for inspiration.

'I wouldn't be helping with the children. No, she wants me to do a sort of survey. On child behaviour. It's just me she's asked, not Maggie or Louise. Apparently she's talked it over

115

with Mrs Philpotts, and she thinks it would be a really worth-
while holiday project for me. There's a chance that my in-
formation might be included in an actual book she's planning
on child psychology. I won't be paid or anything, but I think it
would be worth doing. It's going to be awkward refusing,
especially as Mrs Philpotts is so in favour of the idea. She
recommended me to Mrs Adamson. And it is only in the
afternoons. I can help out in the shop and study and everything in the morning, can't I? Oh Dad, please say I can. I didn't
commit myself, I said I'd have to discuss it with you first, of
course, and Mrs Adamson said that was very sensible but
please, please can I do it?'

It worked.

Chapter 12

I met Richard every single afternoon. At first we went on special outings, but after a while we started going to the derelict house where we'd first said 'I love you.' We found a broken window at the back and climbed in and made the house our own, although the empty VP wine bottles in the corner of the bare living-room showed us that we weren't always the only occupants.

I improved the sleazy little house with imaginary games. Richard's contribution was more practical. He brought a rug, a couple of old cushions, his cassette recorder, cans of coke, crisps and biscuits. I started to get carried away too. I pinched an old glass vase from home and arranged fresh wild flowers in it every day. I brought books and notebooks and drawing things from my room. I sometimes brought the little snow-storm as an ornament. It was like the games of house I'd played years ago with Nicola.

I worried about Nicola. She knew I was seeing Richard and she exploited the situation. She started hinting in front of Mum and Dad, giving me meaningful nudges and nods. She wasn't trying to give me away. She was just enjoying the fact that we had a secret together again.

She wanted so badly to share everything with me. She kept me awake for hours each night, begging me to tell her every little detail about my meetings with Richard. It irritated me. I didn't want her to share Richard even vicariously. I didn't want to tell her about the library at the stately home, the baby elephant at the zoo, the glass of white wine on the boat trip. They were *my* precious days, and I wanted to keep them whole and complete in my memory. When Nicola knew and ex-claimed and chattered then everything became diluted and distorted.

117

I was stupid enough to tell her about the house.

'Where exactly is it? Oh do tell me about it. Couldn't you take me there one day, just to show me what it's like?' Nicola begged. And then, 'What do you *do* there all afternoon?'

'Just mind your own business, will you?'

But Nicola wouldn't. When Richard and I came out of the house the next day I saw Nicola standing at the end of the road. Just standing there gormlessly. She ran round the corner when she saw me, and at home in our bedroom she swore tearfully that she hadn't been anywhere near that road and that I must have been mistaken.

'You liar! You were spying on me, you nosy little beast. If I ever catch you near there again I'll kill you, do you hear me? Just leave me *alone*. It's not my fault you can't make any friends of your own.'

'Yes, I can,' Nicola sobbed, clutching Muffle. 'You're not the only one with a boy-friend, Katherine. I've got one too, if you must know. I shall be seeing a lot of him these holidays. So don't kid yourself I want to spy on you and your boring, common, yobby, fat Richard. I don't care what you do with your boy-friend. I only care about Charles.'

'Charles!'

'His name's Charles Christmas,' she said proudly, wiping her eyes.

'Oh Nicola, really! What a name!'

'I think it's a lovely name.'

'Quite. How old is he then, your Charles?'

'I'm not sure.'

'What school does he go to?'

'He's not a little schoolboy. He works.'

'Where?'

'What do you mean?'

'Where does he work?'

'Well, he doesn't at the moment. He's unemployed. But it's not his fault he's out of work. It's the recession,' she said grandly. 'He might be down on his luck now, so he can't really afford to take me to many places, but in the past he's been very well off indeed. You can tell. Charles is a gentleman.'

I burst out laughing.

118

'You can laugh. You're just jealous because Richard isn't posh.'

'Oh, do stop being so ridiculous, Nicola. We've played too many games together. I know you're making him up.'

'I am not. Charles is real. I swear he is. He's my boy-friend and I love him.'

'Then if he's real let me meet him,' I said cruelly.

'Oh no. I don't want you to meet him. Why should I? You've never introduced me properly to your Richard or invited me along with you. So you jolly well can't meet Charles. He doesn't want to meet you, anyway. I've told him all about you and he says you sound spiteful and stuck up, so there.'

Nicola was being so pathetic that I felt sorry for her. I realised how nasty I'd been to her ever since I'd met Richard. I felt worse when she started bringing little tokens back with her to try to prove to me that Charles existed. She produced a couple of bus tickets and told me about the lovely ride they'd had together. Then she dropped a café bill into my lap, with two meals itemised. She'd obviously picked them up off the pavement somewhere. But the day after Richard bought me my own copy of *The Bell Jar* (he'd come with me to the library and I'd moaned because it wasn't on the shelves and I'd fancied reading it for the fourth or fifth time) Nicola proudly displayed her own paperback. It was an Agatha Christie crime novel, unmistakably brand new.

'See what Charles bought me? You're not the only one to get treats.'

'Where did you get that, Nicola?' I said, shivering.

'I told you. Charles gave it to me.'

'Don't be silly.'

Dad sold some paperbacks in the shop but not this particular sort – and besides, Nicola would never get away with stealing in front of him. But it looked as if she'd stolen from somewhere else. She certainly didn't have enough pocket money to buy it.

'Oh Nic, please, you've got to stop all this,' I said. 'I'm sorry, I know it's half my fault. It was horrible of me showing off like that about Richard. Please don't feel you've got to compete all the time. Be honest with me. Did you take this book from Smiths or what? Because if you try again you'll get caught and

119

just think what Dad would do if he ever knew you'd been shop-lifting.'

I clutched hold of her arm but she shrugged it off.

'You're letting your famous imagination run away with you,' she said coldly. 'I told you, Charles gave it to me as a present.'

'Will you stop going on about this bloody stupid Charles when we both know he doesn't exist!' I shouted. 'I can't bear it when we're not friends. Please let's make it up.'

'I didn't think you wanted me as a friend,' said Nicola. 'You told me to find a proper friend of my own. Well, I have. So hard luck.' She ran out of the room, and wouldn't speak to me any more that day.

I'd kept quiet about Nicola to Richard up till then because I was ashamed of the way I'd behaved. But I was so upset that the next day I couldn't respond properly when he kissed me at our house and eventually I burst into tears.

'Am I that horrible?' said Richard. 'Come on, Katy, tell me what's up.'

So I sobbed it all out while Richard rocked me like a baby.

'I've been such a pig to her, Richard, and yet now when I want to make it up she won't. She just talks maddeningly about her stupid Charles.'

'Are you sure she's making him up?' said Richard. 'She could easily have met up with some boy, especially if she's been hanging around the town a lot.'

'Oh Richard, don't be daft. Nicola couldn't have a boy-friend. She's only thirteen and she's like a great baby. She still has all these cuddly animals in bed with her at night, for goodness' sake.'

'I know a girl of fifteen who does nothing but play pretend games all the time,' said Richard.

'That's different. Anyway, I know when I'm making things up and when I'm not. But I'm not sure if Nicola does. That's what frightens me.'

It had always been easy to convince Nicola that any game was real. Even now, a great girl of thirteen, she still genuinely believed in Sniffle, Woffle and Muffle, and all the Paper People. Only the other day I'd opened up the fashion book and found Patty Pert and all her simpering little friends arranged

120

around an elaborately iced sponge cake that Nicola had cut out of an old magazine. She'd drawn ten candles on the cake, and cut out all sorts of little presents for Patty: a doll, a teddy bear, a pair of stripy socks, some unsuitably sophisticated underwear and a fluffy white kitten with a pink ribbon in its fur. The cut-out kitten was twice the size of little Patty, and in real life would have been as terrifying as a tiger, but Nicola was never deterred by perspective. She'd put my ladies in a folded piece of paper that was supposed to be their house, although their heads stuck out of the red crayoned roof and their feet protruded from the basement. There was no sign of Mr Tremble. After a search amongst Nicola's things I found him imprisoned under a pile of books. She'd pencilled handcuffs round his wrists and a rope around his rain coat. She was obviously determined that Patty wasn't going to get molested on her birthday.

Did she really think Mr Tremble's little paper fingers could tweak plump little Patty?

Did she really think Charles Christmas was trotting round the town with her, taking her for bus rides, treating her to meals, and buying her Agatha Christie paperbacks?

'Why Agatha Christie anyway? Nicola doesn't even like crime novels, they worry her,' I said to Richard. 'What if she tries to steal something else? Do you think it's all my fault?'

'I suppose it's my fault, really. I've taken you away from her. Look, shall we start asking her to come round with us for a bit? We could ask Wendy too. She's been a bit miffed these holidays because I used to do a lot more things with her. My mum was getting on to me only the other day.'

'But I don't want Nicola and Wendy hanging round us, do you?'

'Of course I don't.'

'Why should they be allowed to spoil everything? They're not really our responsibility, are they? Richard, promise me they won't ever come here, to our house. It's just for us, right?'

'Right.'

'Wouldn't it be lovely if we could really live here all the time?'

'Life would be a bit basic,' said Richard. 'No lights. No heating. No cooking facilities. What would we do about grub?'

'Grub! What a horrible word. Do you have to talk like the *Beano*?'

'Sorry, your ladyship.'

'If you mean food, Richard, then that's simple. Fish and chips for every day and we'll have a slap up meal at Albert's every Saturday evening.'

'I'm beginning to like the sound of this. So we're going to live here from now on, are we?' said Richard, pulling me close.

'Yes please.'

'Right. Only we'd better keep up appearances. Hang on.' He fumbled in the pocket of his cords, brought out a bus ticket and started folding it up.

'What are you doing?'

'Wait a minute. You shut your eyes. Properly. Now, hold out your hand. Not that one, your left one.'

He took my hand in his and I felt him pushing gently at my third finger.

'Open your eyes,' Richard whispered.

I was wearing a beautiful bus ticket ring.

'It's lovely,' I said, smiling to show him I knew it was just a joke.

'I wish it was a real ring,' said Richard seriously, lifting my hand up and kissing the paper token. 'We won't have to pretend one day, Katy. It'll be a real ring and we'll have a real house of our own. If that's what you want too.'

'You know it is,' I whispered, and I put my arms round his neck and hugged him determinedly. 'I do love you, Richard. What am I going to do when you go on holiday? How am I going to bear it without you?'

Richard was going to Devon with his family. The Friday before he went off, I risked the Miss Hyde alibi again and went out with him for a meal at Albert's. I had corn on the cob and hamburger with bacon and pickle and a baked potato with melted butter and a side salad and then a raspberry sorbet with a wafer biscuit in the shape of a fan. I ate up every mouthful but I could have been eating Nicola's paper food.

My chair was very near Richard's, but I kept edging even closer. I held his hand tightly under the table. After our lovely meal we went to our house but it was horribly different in the dark. We couldn't see where we were going, I tripped twice on the stairs even with Richard holding me, it was cold and chilly in our bedroom and the smell from the blocked lavatory bloomed in the dark. I clung to Richard for comfort. He kissed me and told me he loved me again and again but I couldn't relax. His voice sounded frighteningly loud in the silent shell of the house, but it was even worse when he was quiet. Every tap and rustle and creak made me think drunks or vagrants or gangs of yobs were creeping up on us.

'I was silly to bring you here. I'm sorry, Katy,' Richard said, sighing.

'I wanted to come, you know I did. I'm just being silly. I'm spoiling our house, making it all creepy and horrible, but I can't stop it,' I said tearfully.

'You're not spoiling it. The first day I get back from my holiday we'll come here in the afternoon and it will be all sunny and friendly and perfect, you'll see,' Richard promised.

I did my best to believe him.

I didn't know what to do with myself for the next two weeks. I wanted to make it up with Nicola and do things with her but she still wouldn't have anything to do with me.

'Richard's on holiday, isn't he!' she guessed. 'I knew you'd do this. I knew you'd come round me and expect me to be all over you again. Well, hard luck. Charles *isn't* on holiday. I'm busy seeing him every day. And I'm afraid you can't come trailing round after us. You'd just be in the way. So you'll just have to amuse yourself, Katherine. You should try to make a few friends, then you wouldn't be at such a loose end the minute your precious Richard deserts you.'

She nodded at me triumphantly as she bustled round our bedroom, tidying up before she went out. Her mottled thighs showed as she bent over to retrieve one of her animals. She was getting fatter than ever. Her denim skirt and T-shirt were much too tight for her. She'd started tying her hair up in a scrappy sort of bun because she thought it made her look older, but it left her face too exposed. It was so large and pink and shiny, like a boiled ham. In ten years' time she wouldn't be Nicola at all, she'd just be a clone of our mother.

As I watched her she dug into her tight pocket and stuck a toffee into her mouth. She was already chewing on another.

'For goodness' sake, Nic, you've only just had breakfast. You're getting so *fat*.'

She stood still, chewing obstinately.

'What makes you think you've got the right to criticise me?' she said. 'You keep on, nag, moan, whine, you never let up. You do it to everyone. I don't know how Richard can stand it. He's probably glad to be on holiday so he can have a rest from you. What makes you think you've got this divine right to tell people what to do? Do you think you're perfect?'

'Look, I only – I was trying – '

'Listen to me. You're not so great, you know. All right, you're a phenomenal brainbox and you've got your fancy scholarship and you go to a posh school and you're going to get all those boring A grades in your O levels – '

'No, I'm – '

'Will you *listen*! That's just typical. You always want to say your piece and never give anyone else a try. What's so great about being clever? What makes you think you're a big success? You go on about me not having friends but you haven't either, have you? And you're always hateful about the way I look and yet you're no oil painting. I might be a bit plump but I'd sooner be that than all skinny and scrawny like you. And at least I'm getting a proper figure. You're as flat as a pancake, it's pathetic. Yet I don't go on at you all the time, telling you to eat more or exercise or whatever. And look at your awful hair. You're forever telling me that mine looks a mess and that it doesn't suit me to put it up and that I ought to wash it more often – but I could carry on for hours about your frizzy great mop. You're a mess and I'm glad I'm me and not you.'

She walked out of the room, unwrapping another toffee and stuffing it in her mouth. I stood still, hearing her voice going on and on. I felt my face pucker. It was the first time Nicola had ever made me cry. I ended up lying on her bed with Sniffle, Woffle and Muffle, howling.

Chapter 13

I'd never been so bored in all my life. I had to go out every day from one to half past five to keep up the myth that I was helping at the nursery school. I couldn't suddenly invent a holiday. I'd taken great pains to convince Dad that the nursery stayed open all through the summer, unlike normal schools, because it catered for working mothers. I had no idea whether this was true or not, and didn't dare check. I prayed Dad wouldn't check either. I knew I was taking an enormous risk but when I was seeing Richard every day it seemed worth it.

Without him I was lost. Nicola and I were barely speaking, even in front of Mum and Dad. She rushed off every day to keep her tryst with her imaginary Charles. I looked out for her as I trailed round the town by myself, but I never saw her.

I had no idea what to do with myself. I realised what it must have been like for Nicola playing truant all these months. I spent the first afternoon going round the shops, the second in the library – but then I ran out of ideas. I had no money to go to the pictures or to take a bus ride. I walked in the park and down by the river but it was horribly lonely. Everyone else seemed paired like Ark animals. Even the ducks swam in twos.

I tried going to our house one day but I hated it. It was frightening even in the daylight, and I found fish and chip wrappings and empty cans of beer strewn on the living-room floor.

I stayed away after that, often spending the whole afternoon walking round uninteresting back streets playing counting games. I counted red curtains and blue vases and yellow doors and green gates and purple cars until my eyes ached and they all blurred into a garish rainbow. I didn't care how many there were. It was the counting itself that mattered, because it stopped me thinking. Now I was no longer absorbed in

Richard, O level worries spiralled my brain day and night. It wouldn't be long before I got the results – and then oh God, oh God, what was I going to do?

I got my school books out sometimes when I was at home, because Dad kept nagging that I mustn't let my brain go soft during the holidays, but I couldn't read more than a paragraph before the words blurred. I kept secretly reading the passage in *The Bell Jar* where Esther can't read anything except sensational newspapers. I tried glancing at the *Sun* in the shop, and it was true, the words didn't waver once.

So what was happening to me? Was I going mad too? Esther tried to commit suicide but I was far too cowardly. Perhaps I could run away instead? But where would I go, what would I live on, how could I manage?

I couldn't eat properly either. I felt slightly sick all the time. I knew I couldn't be pregnant but it preyed on my mind all the same. One breakfast time, when the sausages were greasier than ever, I only just made it to the bathroom, and when I dragged myself back, shivering, Mum took one look at me and sent me to bed.

I pulled the covers over my head thankfully and tried to blot everything out. I fell asleep and didn't wake up until Mum came creaking into the room a couple of hours later.

'Sorry dear. Go back to sleep if you want. I just thought I'd better see how you were.'

I sat up uncertainly. Mum peered at me.

'You still look ever so peaky. I'll bring you a spot of lunch on a tray in half an hour. A nice bit of plaice, you ought to be able to keep that down. And I should stay home from the nursery today. I'll give Mrs Adamson a ring, shall I?'

'No! No, I feel much better now, honestly. I'll go to the nursery.'

'I don't think that's a very good idea, Katherine, especially if you've got some kind of bug. You don't want to pass it on to any of the little ones, do you?'

'I haven't got a bug. It was just those disgusting sausages. I keep telling you, I can't eat them.'

'It's not just the sausages,' said Mum, and she sat down heavily on the end of the bed, nearly capsizing both of us. 'What *is* the matter, dear?'

126

'Nothing.'

Mum sighed. 'Look, I know you haven't got a very high opinion of me, but I'm not stupid. There's something wrong. It's not doing you any good keeping it to yourself. Can't I help?'

'No, you can't,' I said rudely.

Mum flushed and shook her head sorrowfully.

'Even Nicola's not herself. What have you two quarrelled about?'

'Nothing.'

'She's as stubborn as you are, she won't tell me a thing. It's always been so nice, that the two of you have been so close. Can't you make it up with her?'

'I've tried. But she doesn't want to.'

Mum frowned and twisted her head sideways, obviously not believing me.

'Really. She doesn't want anything to do with me.'

'What have you done to upset her so?'

'She just doesn't want to be friends with me any more,' I said. 'Do shut up about it, Mum.'

'Oh well.' She looked at me carefully. 'How are your other friends?'

'Which friends?' I said, swinging my legs out of bed. 'I'd better get dressed now.'

'That boy who came into the shop. Richard,' Mum persisted.

I busied myself putting on my socks and shoes, keeping my head well bent.

'He's – he's all right,' I mumbled.

'Do you see a lot of him?' Mum asked.

'I haven't seen him for a while,' I said truthfully.

'I see,' said Mum, sounding relieved. But as she went out of my bedroom she added, 'I thought he seemed a very nice boy.'

I lay back on my bed, basking in what she'd said. Oh, he was a very nice boy, the most wonderful boy in all the world. He'd even managed to find a way of sending me a postcard.

'Dear Katy, I'm having a lovely time and the weather is fine but my brother is being a bore this holiday. He is just moping around fed up because he's missing his girl-friend. Hope to see you soon, Love from Wendy.'

Dad had snatched the postcard out of my hand before I'd even had a chance to read it properly. He questioned me for half an hour about this new friend Wendy. If she was one of the girls at school, why hadn't I mentioned her before? What was she doing writing me postcards? What sort of girl was she?

I got up and pretended to go to the nursery school that afternoon, even though I really felt dreadful. I was sick behind a bush in the park, wasting the nice bit of plaice. I felt better for a little while, but then my stomach started to clench, and I ended up spending most of the afternoon having diarrhea in the ladies public lavatories.

I dragged myself home feeling martyred. Dad was in the shop serving two little boys.

'Make up your blooming minds then. Six raspberry chews? Look, I'm not messing about picking out the red ones, you'll have to have assorted or go without. Katherine, don't go. I want you. Here's your chews – and get your hands out of that jar, you mucky little devil. If you want a lolly I'll get it for you. I don't want those germy hands contaminating my stock, thank you very much.'

The little boys waited until they were outside the door and yelled abuse, telling Dad just what he could do with his lollies.

'Ignorant little guttersnipes,' said Dad, savagely screwing the lid back on the lolly jar. 'Now Katherine. Miss Hyde came in the shop this afternoon.'

His words were like blows in my sore stomach.

'She wanted to have a word with you,' said Dad. He'd got the lid on the wrong thread and jerked at it impotently. 'Damn daft object. *Go* on, will you?' He gave it one more wrench and then slammed it down onto the counter with such force that the plastic buckled.

Was he furious with me or the boys or the sweet jar? I nibbled at the skin on my bottom lip although I knew it infuriated him.

'Will you stop standing like a zombie eating bits of yourself?' he said. He made swatting gestures at my lips. I dodged back, thinking he was attacking me.

'What's up with you? Stop *doing* that. Yes, Miss Hyde wants you to go to tea with her tomorrow.'

'Oh,' I said faintly.

'That's right. Tea again. I don't know what's got into the woman. She must think very highly of you to go to all this trouble. I thanked her very much.'

'You thanked her?'

'Have you gone deaf or something? Deaf or daft. Stop looking so witless. You're meant to be the bright one of the family. So look it, girl, look it! Of course I thanked Miss Hyde. Don't you think I've got any manners? I said I was very touched that she asked you to tea so often. It's very good of her to give you all this extra free tuition.'

'What did she say?'

'She looked a bit taken aback, I must say. Probably not used to gratitude. Most parents don't take an interest in their children, do they? Anyway, you're to go there at half past five. You'll have to go straight from the nursery school. I explained you might be a bit late. She didn't seem to know much about your project.'

'Oh, it was Mrs Adamson's idea. She probably wouldn't have discussed it with Miss Hyde,' I said.

My stomach was churning so violently I had to cut the conversation short and run to the lavatory.

I sat there long after it was necessary, going over what Dad had said again and again. He really didn't seem to suspect a thing. But what had he said to Miss Hyde? Did she suspect anything? And oh God, I didn't *want* to have tea with her. I thought of her big, shining nose, her botany wool jumper, her baggy tweed skirt. I didn't want to sit on her black, fur fabric pouffe and eat Scotch pancakes and talk Literature.

But I didn't dare stay away. At half past five the next day I walked down the steps to her dank basement flat and presented myself to her.

'Hello, Katherine. Do come in. How delightfully prompt you are! I can hear the half-hour just striking, can't you?'

I muttered politely, and we sat down at her table. Scotch pancakes again, the fruity sort this time, and Spam sandwiches and a plate of elderly custard creams. There wasn't much to choose between Mum's teas and Miss Hyde's. I started eating warily, telling her that I was just getting over a stomach bug and didn't have much of an appetite.

'Yes, your father told me,' said Miss Hyde.

129

I stopped chewing and looked at her. She looked back at me. Her face gave nothing away. I hoped mine didn't either. She had her hair cut short in a new style which made her look younger. She was probably only in her twenties although she dressed like a middle-aged woman. She was wearing dreadful beige polyster trousers today, with great flapping legs.

'He's obviously very proud of you,' said Miss Hyde.

I shrugged uncomfortably.

'Still, he's got every reason to be proud,' she said, smiling.

A currant from her Scotch pancake was wedged between her front teeth. I probed my own teeth with my tongue. 'He's not going to be proud for very long because I know I've failed all my O levels.' But I didn't say it out loud. I couldn't tell her, even though she'd find out soon enough.

'How have you been getting on with your reading?'

'Not terribly well, so far,' I said. 'I haven't had much time, honestly.'

'Yes, your father said you were – '

'I started *What Maisie Knew* but I couldn't seem to get on with it,' I interrupted. 'But I read *Washington Square* instead and I enjoyed that. I was interested in the way James writes about Catherine.'

I hadn't read *Washington Square* either, but it had been adapted into a radio play a while ago and I remembered the plot. I knew that would safely divert her. She started a long eulogy on Henry James, and I nodded and smiled in appropriate places. She lent me her own copy of *The Portrait of a Lady* and then she started on George Eliot and *Daniel Deronda* and *Mill on the Floss* and then brought Shakespeare into the discussion and I didn't have to worry any more, she could always talk about him for hours.

I usually wanted to *listen* for hours. Miss Hyde was frumpy and foolish, but she was a marvellous English teacher. She usually made me feel I was soaring into a whole new universe of images and ideas. But I remained earthbound today. I couldn't concentrate on what she was saying. There didn't seem any point to any of it. I didn't care what Henry James and George Eliot and Shakespeare wrote about love.

I wanted to think about my love. I stared at Miss Hyde and pitied her. She only knew about love in books. I was only

130

fifteen and I had failed my O levels and mucked up my whole academic future, but I knew about love firsthand.

I thought of Richard. He wasn't a character in a book or a play. I hadn't invented him either. He was real, he was real, he was real.

'Katherine?'

She'd stopped speaking.

'Sorry? I – I was just trying to think of a particular quotation.'

She didn't look convinced.

'Katherine, is there anything the matter?'

'No.'

'You seem a bit preoccupied.'

'Sorry. I suppose it's because I've been taking it easy recently. My brain's gone a bit soft.'

'I think your brain's working perfectly,' said Miss Hyde, removing her glasses and polishing them with a hankie.

She looked bare without them, as if she'd taken her clothes off too. There were two mauve dents at the bridge of her big nose where her glasses rubbed. She put the glasses back on with a little wince. She saw me properly again and smiled.

'Don't worry. I'm not going to pry. Maybe it's a good thing you're not concentrating on academic work at the moment. I think you've done rather too much studying in the past. I've appreciated it, of course. It's lovely for me having such a rewarding pupil but I'm not sure it's necessarily lovely for you.' She gathered up the books she was going to lend me for the holidays. 'Borrow these later, when you're back at school. Have a little rest from literature now.'

I was disconcerted. How much had she guessed? Did she know I was in love? Did she realise I'd been using her as an alibi? Did she mind?

But I didn't care about Miss Hyde any more. I only cared about Richard. I whispered his name over and over again on my way home. He was coming back on Saturday. I'd be seeing him soon, we'd go to our house, and somehow it would all be special again and nothing else would matter in the whole world.

Chapter 14

Richard came into the shop at half past five on Saturday, just as Dad was closing. For one extraordinary second I didn't recognise him. I suppose it wasn't so surprising. He was tanned a glossy toffee-apple brown and his hair was bleached to a glamorous platinum blond. He was wearing clothes I'd never seen before, a navy and white striped T-shirt and white jeans. They showed off his tan perfectly.

He looked like a stranger, not my Richard. I wanted to duck down behind the counter and hide. My hair was pulled back into an ugly pony-tail because Dad had started moaning about hygiene in a shop that sold food. My T-shirt had stretched in the wash so that the sleeves were like large bells tolling against my skinny arms.

But Richard smiled at me as if he thought me perfect.

Dad saw the smile and squinted at Richard in a threatening manner.

'Yes? We're just closing, so make your mind up quickly.'

Richard went over to where I was standing and pretended to look at the chocolate bars in front of me. He chose blindly, his hand moving at random, while he looked at me and mouthed 'I love you'. I didn't dare try mouthing anything back because of Dad, but I could feel myself glowing. My heart pumped my blood round my body at an alarming rate, a scarlet Niagara surging inside me.

Dad sniffed suspiciously.

'I know you, don't I?' he said.

I clutched the edge of the counter, but Richard turned round calmly.

'Yes, that's right, Mr Petworthy. I took over young Mark Mason's paper round for a few days, remember?'

'Oh yes. Well, I hope he's not going to go skiving off again.

132

I'll not stand for it, you know. I've got boys and girls queuing up to work for me,' Dad lied.

Richard nodded tactfully and turned back to me. He held out his chocolate bars, touching the palm of my hand with the tips of his fingers.

'I'll have these please.'

But Dad was edging round the counter.

'I'll take them. Katherine, go upstairs and help your mother. Come on, young man, where's your money? I'm about to close the till so you're holding me up.'

As I went through to the back obediently I turned and looked at Richard. He winked at me and for once I didn't mind.

When Dad came and sat down to his maccaroni cheese ten minutes later he was still frowning.

'I didn't like the way that boy looked at you, Katherine,' he said, tucking into his tea. 'The nerve of some of these yobs nowadays. Don't just stand there looking gormless when they make eyes at you. Act like a lady and show your disdain.'

'Yes Dad.' I kept my eyes on my plate.

'You don't want to encourage louts like that, do you?' said Dad.

'No Dad.' I shook my head solemnly – and Nicola tittered.

Dad peered at her.

'What are you snorting about?'

'Nothing,' Nicola stammered.

Dad's head swivelled back to me.

'What's going on? Come on, you needn't think you can keep anything from me. Katherine? What have you been up to?'

'I haven't been up to anything.'

'Then why are you and your sister looking at each other like that? Have you been doing something you shouldn't? Have you been playing up to any of these yobbos, is that it?' Dad threw his knife and fork onto his plate, spattering the table-cloth with cheese sauce.

'Careful, dear, that cloth's clean on,' said Mum. 'Nicola, get the J-cloth from the kitchenette. Wring it out first.'

Nicola lumbered off.

'Honestly Dad, can you see me talking to any of those boys?' I said quickly. 'I think they're awful. Of course I don't want to encourage them. But I get so embarrassed sometimes when they look at me. Not that they often do. But the other day out in the street this awful boy gave me a wolf whistle and I just about died. I blushed and started running away, making a perfect fool of myself, and Nicola saw and teased me about it.'

Dad was safely diverted.

'Who whistled at you? Damn cheek! You should have come and told me straight away, I'd have soon settled his hash. Who was it, one of our customers? Not that fair boy who came in just now?'

'No, it was just a silly little kid. Wasn't he, Nicola?'

She was back with the J-cloth. Her hands shook as she rubbed at the stain.

'Yes, honestly, Dad,' she gabbled.

'Watch what you're doing. Get your big elbow out of my face. Can't it wait until I've finished my tea? All this fuss about a minute splash. Sit *down*, Nicola, and stop dabbing that dish-rag everywhere. Ye gods, I've never seen anyone so clumsy. Never mind two left feet, you've got two left arms as well.'

When Dad had finished having a go at her I got Nicola on her own and started on her myself.

'You laughed like that on purpose!' I hissed, not sure whether I believed it or not.

Nicola cringed away from me. 'I didn't, I didn't! I couldn't stop myself. It was nerves, you know the way I get.'

I knew, but it was satisfactory to have Nicola in my power again.

I couldn't wait to see Richard properly. I rushed out on Sunday afternoon the minute Mum and Dad went upstairs. Nicola didn't attempt to follow me. Richard was waiting for me down the road, as I'd hoped – but he had Wendy with him again.

I was furious. I had been longing to go to our house where we could be private together. Why on earth had Richard brought that stupid little Wendy along on our first proper day together? She was very brown too, showing off her tan in a vulgar pair of tight, white shorts and a pink halter top. It had nothing to halt, so it looked ridiculous. Wendy's doll, Madeleine, wore a pair of large blue knickers and a beret crammed down over her bedraggled curls.

Wendy smiled at me as if we were old friends.

134

'Watcha, Katy. Aren't I brown? Do you like my top? It's new. Look, I've brought my doll. Are you going to make her talk again? She fell in the sea on holiday and it's made her go all squelchy inside, listen.'

I didn't want to listen. I didn't want to have anything to do with this boring little girl. Richard was smiling at us both in an irritating, paternal fashion. He didn't asked me if I minded going to the park. We set off in that direction, regardless.

Wendy wouldn't even run ahead. She tucked her sticky little hand through my arm and skipped along beside me, nattering a lot of rubbish. Her bitten finger nails were painted scarlet. She asked me three times if I liked the colour of her nail varnish. I didn't like it, I didn't like anything about her, but I smiled and nodded and twittered rubbish back.

I hoped Richard would see that I was making a huge effort for his sake, but he seemed under the impression that I was enjoying Wendy's company. When at long last we got rid of her on the swings he looked astonished when I said, 'Why on earth did you bring her?'

'You don't really mind, do you? You both get on so well. Wendy kept on at me. She loved the idea of me sending a postcard to you in her name. She bought you a stick of rock out of her own pocket-money as a holiday present, but then she got hungry in the car going home and ended up eating half of it. She still wanted to give you the sucked remains, but I managed to talk her out of it.'

I refused to laugh. I was sick of being charming.

'I wanted to go to our house, Richard,'

'So did I. Still, we can go all next week, can't we?' Richard said brightly.

I glared at him. I was furious with him and yet his lovely brown arms and his bleached hair and his tight white jeans made me ache to have him hold me.

'You've had Wendy for the past fortnight. Surely you could have got rid of her today?' I said sulkily.

'Not without being really mean to her. She's only a little kid. It's ever so easy to hurt her feelings.'

'Look, I've got a sister too. I hurt her feelings all the time.'

Richard burst out laughing.

'Just because you're a mean old ratbag to your sister I don't

135

see why I should act the same to mine,' he said, giving me a big hug. 'Cheer up, Katy. Come on, smile. Little smile for Richard, eh? Is that cross little mouth twitching?'

He started tickling me under the chin. I pulled away from him, not wanting to be treated like a two-year-old, even though I was aware I was behaving like one.

'I know something that might make you smile,' said Richard, refusing to give up. 'Wendy's holiday present to you might be a bit of a wash-out, but mine's still intact.' He fumbled in the pocket of his jeans and brought out a little packet wrapped in pink tissue paper. I held it on the palm of my hand, my heart thudding. It was a ring. It had to be a ring. I couldn't think of anything else that size. But why give it to me here, in the park, with Wendy and these other children milling around us?

'Shall I wait and open it in our house tomorrow?' I whispered, closing my fingers round the little package.

Richard looked disappointed.

'No, open it now! Come on, I want to see if it fits.'

So I opened it up with Wendy gawping at us on the swings and a toddler standing beside us, picking his nose. It was a ring. A little silver ring, twisted into the shape of a wishbone.

'Oh Richard, it's lovely!'

But it wasn't, it wasn't. It wasn't beautiful or unusual. I'd seen hundreds like it before. It wasn't special in any way.

'I thought you'd like it,' said Richard proudly. 'Shall I put it on for you?'

But he didn't put it on my left hand this time. He tried my right, only it didn't sit properly on my ring finger.

'Your fingers are so thin. And I got the smallest size,' he said, looking at his precious ring in consternation.

'It does fit. Look, on this finger,' I said, putting it on my forefinger.

'But it's the wrong finger, isn't it?' Richard said doubtfully.

'I told you it wouldn't fit her,' Wendy called.

'It fits,' I said firmly, holding Richard's hand. 'It fits and it's lovely. It's the best ring in all the world because you chose it specially for me.'

136

Richard looked at me lovingly, but Wendy came running from her swing.

'He didn't choose it, I did,' she said, swaggering.

'Shut up, Wendy,' said Richard.

I didn't mind. Richard looked flushed and foolish but that made me love him more.

I couldn't wait to go to our house with him.

There were more empty beer cans and the smell from the lavatory was worse, but I didn't care. It was Richard who wrinkled his nose.

'It doesn't half pong in here.'

'Richard!'

'What? Oh sorry, Madam Muck. My *Beano* vocabulary again. Beg pardon, I'm sure. Very remiss of me.'

I didn't know whether he was deliberately saying things to irritate me or not.

'Stop it! And stop moaning about the smell. Come to our bedroom.'

'You shameless hussy,' said Richard, wiggling his eyebrows up and down stupidly.

I didn't want him to joke and mess about. I struggled to stay in control of my temper. I didn't want to start nagging at him again. I wanted everything to be beautiful and perfect and loving between us. So I took his hand and led him up the disintegrating stairs to our bedroom. There were no beer cans there, thank goodness. The smell was there, but fainter. I kissed Richard and he kissed me back, serious at last, and I was soon only aware of the warm, honey smell of his flesh. It was strange seeing him toasted a different colour. I made him undress and admired him. He was endearingly bashful at first, but then his confidence increased and he started showing off, flexing his muscles and posing. I laughed at him and he didn't like that and started tickling me and then we were kissing. Much more than kissing. But eventually Richard pushed me away.

'I'm sorry,' he whispered.

I gave a little grunt, not wanting to speak.

'Katy? Katy, we couldn't. It would be madness. You know it would.'

'I don't see why,' I mumbled.

'You don't want to end up pregnant, do you?'

'Of course not. But there's such a thing as contraception, isn't there?'

He stared at me. His hair was rumpled and sticking up childishly. He had one leg in his jeans and he looked ridiculous.

'You mean you could go on the Pill?' he said uncertainly.

'Oh, it has to be my responsibility, does it?' I snapped, because I knew I didn't dare approach a doctor.

Richard was balanced on one leg, still displaying his cheap, patterned underpants. They were covered with arrows and exclamation marks.

'For God's sake, do you have to wear those?'

'Well, I'd look daft without any,' said Richard. 'What's up with my pants? Why do you have to keep getting at me, Katy?'

'They're revolting! Crude and vulgar and ridiculous.'

'Thanks very much. They were a birthday present from my brother,' said Richard.

He looked at me triumphantly, expecting me to bluster and apologise, but I didn't see why I should.

'Then he is probably as crude and vulgar and ridiculous as your underwear,' I said.

Richard pulled on his jeans hurriedly. He fumbled with his zip, his hands shaking.

'Thanks very much,' he said, attempting sarcasm. 'That makes me feel really great.'

I realised I had seriously hurt him.

'What on earth are you so upset about?'

'I'm not upset,' Richard said shakily, pulling on his T-shirt. 'What do you think of my shirt, eh? My Mum bought it for me on holiday. Would you care to criticise that too?'

'I can't understand you. Are you upset because I criticise your clothes or members of your family?'

'I am *not* upset,' said Richard, pulling on a sock and getting it inside out.

'You're practically in tears! And I don't see why. I don't give a damn who criticises my clothes or my family. I am perfectly aware that I have the most hideous clothes. They are ancient and shabby and home-made and pathetic. I hate every single garment I own. I hate my family too.'

138

'No you don't.'

'I do. My mother is a great fat stupid cow. My father is a bad tempered bully. My sister is an immature, cowardly idiot. I hate all of them.' I was shaking too.

'I don't believe you mean that. And even if you do, I still care about my family,' said Richard, ready to go although we usually stayed at our house all the afternoon.

'You're telling me. I'm sick of hearing about them. It makes me want to vomit, all this Happy Family lark. Look at the way you pander to Wendy, letting her practically rule your life. It's a wonder you deigned to meet me at all yesterday.'

'Don't be stupid.'

'Stop telling me I'm stupid. It makes me so mad. What gives you the right to call me stupid? You're the one who's bloody stupid.'

My voice echoed relentlessly in the hushed house. I shut my eyes, the blood beating in my lids.

'I didn't mean it,' I whispered. 'I'm sorry. Oh Richard, I'm sorry, I'm sorry.'

I opened my eyes and saw he was crying.

Chapter 15

I tried hard to make it up. I was good at getting round people and I knew the roles to play with Richard. I was almost motherly at first, putting my arms round him and rocking him and letting him cry. When he was comforted but starting to feel ashamed of his tears I made myself cry, behaving like a lost little girl, so that he could start to feel protective and forgiving. I did it and it worked and we ended up vowing a deeper love than ever, but all the time I knew I was manipulating Richard. I couldn't help resenting him for being so gullible. I wanted him to see through my little games and despise me for them. I wanted him to be able to manipulate me.

It was hard coming to terms with the real Richard. While he'd been away on holiday I'd been making him up to be so different. I'd concentrated on all the sweet, imaginative, tender things he'd said or done. I'd deliberately forgotten all the winks and slang and the childish messing about that irritated me so much. The Richard inside my head was as much a pretend person as Nicola's Charles Christmas.

The real Richard looked glossier, of course, but his tan quickly yellowed and he had a disastrous haircut. His mother had nagged him into going to a barber's, although I loved the way his hair fell softly forward into his eyes. The barber lopped off the floppy part I loved and left unsightly stubble. The sheared hair took away all the balance of his face. It made his nose look bulbous, his ears enormous. His newly exposed neck looked red and raw like something in a butcher's shop.

'Sorry about my hair,' Richard said nervously, as soon as he saw me.

'What do you mean? It's quite nice,' I said, determined to be kind. My voice lacked conviction all the same.

I hoped I would soon get used to it but it seemed to make a

140

ridiculous difference. I couldn't glance casually at Richard any more. I didn't see *him*, I just saw his awful hair. It was easier than ever to be irritable with him because he looked so awful.

I despised myself for my attitude. I knew that six centimetres of hair shouldn't make the slightest difference to my feelings – but they *did*.

Every day when I went to meet Richard I vowed that I would keep my temper and be really nice to him but I rarely managed it. Sometimes I'd snap at him the minute I saw him. I wished that he'd snap back. I wished he'd get so fed up with me he'd retaliate fiercely. But he was hopeless, as soft as sponge. He'd often apologise when it was all my fault, just like Nicola. It made me feel so mean and guilty and then I was even nastier.

'Why on earth do you put up with me?' I asked him.

'Because I love you,' said Richard.

'I don't see why. What is it about me that you love? I'm horrible. I don't even look nice. And inside I'm worse. Don't look at me with your eyes all blurred with love. Focus them, Richard. See me properly.'

He took me literally and blinked, exasperating me even more.

'I love you,' he said desperately.

'Tell me why though, don't just keep parroting it to me.'

'I love you because . . . I just do.'

I sighed and turned away from him, screwing up my face in frustration.

'Can't you even manage one reason?'

'Yes, of course I can. You're . . . you're very attractive.'

'For God's sake, I'm not. I'm hideous. And anyway, what a dull, flaccid sort of word. Attractive. It's meaningless.'

'Well, you're funny and odd and different.'

'Yes, but you've already said that. Many times. The meaning's got squeezed out of the words. You've got to find some new ones now.'

'I haven't got any words. It's all right for you. You keep giving me all these orders and it just makes me panic and I can't think of anything.'

'I know. But why do you let me? Why don't you tell me to shut up? Stop me being so hateful.'

'I don't know how. I don't want to get at you. I love you,

141

Katy. I just want us to be happy together. I don't see why you have to keep picking all these arguments.'

'I don't see why either,' I said, and I hunched into a ball and started to cry.

But I still wasn't acting spontaneously. I was forcing the tears, deliberately curling up small, so that Richard could cope by comforting me.

He wasn't stupid, *I* had been stupid to suggest he was – and yet I seemed to be so much cleverer than him all the same. But I wasn't clever. I wasn't intellectually gifted any more. When my O level results came – oh God, only days now – everyone else would know too. If only I'd never been clever. If I'd been just average, like Nicola, then no one would expect me to get those impossible eleven A grades. Why had I struggled so hard to perpetuate this awful myth of my giftedness? I'd convinced Dad, I'd convinced everyone at Lady Margaret Lancaster's, I'd even convinced myself.

I'd started to realise the truth last year when I started on my O level syllabus. It became more obvious this year, especially when I did the mocks. I'd passed them, I'd got the A grades, but it had been such a desperate struggle. When I was little coming top in all my exams had been easy. It was simply a matter of learning all the facts properly and then setting them out neatly on the exam paper. It wasn't really anything to do with intelligence or ability. All it involved was a bit of hard work and a good memory. If I'd been studying for only five or six O levels then the same system would have worked impeccably. But it was impossible revising for eleven academic subjects, especially the ones that were all difficult details and diagrams, like Geography and Biology. I'd studied for ten or twelve hours at a time all over the Christmas holidays, muttering facts feverishly even when I was sitting on the lav or lying in bed. I dreamt each subject every night, waking up tense and sweating, straining for the right answer.

My brain felt as if it was being blown up like a balloon. My eyes grew hot and sore with all the reading. I fell asleep over my books and yet at nights I couldn't get to sleep for hours.

I hardly slept at all the whole time I was taking my mocks. I stumbled around as if I was walking in a fog. I felt so awful every morning that I could barely grope my way out of bed. My insides seemed fogged up too, so that I could hardly eat anything, and I was sick when I tried. I shivered as I walked to school, I yawned compulsively throughout every assembly, I couldn't hear properly when the teachers talked – but I was all right every time I sat down at the hard little desk in the Gym to do each exam. The terror seemed to trigger my brain. It lit up like a lighthouse, shining powerfully through the fog. I read the questions and mentally assembled each carton of relevant facts. I put them together in my head, a neat jigsaw, and copied it down on paper. I did it eleven times for the eleven exams and I passed every one with the highest grade. I was the only girl in my class to get A grades in every single exam. The other girls groaned and said it wasn't fair.

'After all, it's easy for old brainbox Katherine. She's so brilliant she doesn't even have to try.'

But it wasn't easy, it was the hardest thing I'd ever done. I was ill for weeks afterwards with a sore throat that developed into glandular fever. Mum said it was because I hadn't been eating properly and Dad said it was because I hadn't been having early nights. I knew it was because of the fear growing inside me. It had been too difficult. I couldn't do it again in June. My brain could only expand so far. It couldn't cope any longer.

I tried, of course. I revised constantly, at home and at school. I sat at my desk and stared at my books, but the words were meaningless hieroglyphics. I read each sentence again and again, I muttered the words under my breath, I even tried pointing underneath them like a beginner reader, but I couldn't get them into my closed brain. I was horribly aware of the class-room clock ticking away relentlessly, every minute bringing the exams nearer and nearer.

But I still thought that somehow it would be all right when I actually sat down to do the first exam. But it wasn't, it wasn't. I stared at the paper and read the instructions carefully, the way I'd been taught, and then I read the first question and my heart started pounding so violently I expected it to come bursting bloodily through my white school blouse. I couldn't do it! I didn't know what they were talking about. I read the next question and the next, and they all seemed as bad. What did they *mean*?

143

I could hear the other girls picking up their pens all around me, shifting in their chairs as they started writing busily. I sat unable to move, staring at the exam paper, knowing I couldn't do it.

I attempted it of course. I worked my way methodically through each question and I ended up with the requisite number of answers on my little booklet of paper, but I knew they weren't good enough. I'd lost the ability to find the right facts and fit them together. Half the pieces were missing and the rest wouldn't slot into place.

I didn't even tell anyone what was happening. After each exam the girls poured out of the Gym, laughing and groaning theatrically, and then they'd get together in little groups and go over the whole paper, comparing answers, thumbing through text books. I didn't join in any of the sessions. I hid in the cloakrooms, sitting on the lavatory with my head in my hands.

I heard some of the girls talking about me once when they were all combing their hair at the mirror and I was lurking in my cramped cubicle.

'Do you know who really makes me sick? Katherine Petworthy. The way she just stalks off after each exam, her head in the air! Stuck up little swot. She'll have got boring A grades in every single subject again. *And* she's only fifteen. Doesn't it make you ill?'

'Yes, but who'd want to be Katherine Petworthy, for Heaven's sake?'

'Me! My father promised me twenty pounds for every A grade I get. Imagine eleven. That's . . . er . . . .'

'I don't think you'll be getting an A in Maths, that's for sure! £220, dummy. Oh, but seriously – that's all she's got going for her, her brains. I mean, you wouldn't want to *look* like her, would you?'

'And that voice! The way she says some words when she's not thinking. What was it she said the other day? It wasn't as obvious as dropping an aitch. I know, she said something was ever so something or other, and she sounded so Cockney it wasn't true.'

'Well, she is a bit common. I know she really fancies herself and she's supposed to be sitting for Oxbridge when she's
144

seventeen but she's certainly nothing special. You know what her father is, don't you?'

'What? Do tell. A dustman? Railway porter? Lavatory attendant?'

'A newsagent.'

'He's not!'

'He is, he's our newsagent, as a matter of fact. And a tedious little man he is too, forever sending rude notes to my father about settling the bloody bill. I once went into the shop for some sweets or something when I was in uniform and he practically wet his knickers. "My daughter Katherine goes to Lady Margaret Lancaster's too," he said. Really proud of his Katherine, he is.'

'*Ever* so proud.'

They shrieked with laughter while I stayed crouched behind the door. I should have had the courage to go out and face them. I should have slapped all their silly, snobbish faces. No, I should have looked at them all scornfully and walked away with my head held high. But I was too cowardly to do anything but snivel silently. I knew I didn't fit in, I knew none of them really liked me, but I hadn't realised just how much they hated me. They were right. All I had were my brains. Only they'd stopped working properly and I was nothing without them. I was just an ugly, common little joke.

But I had Richard, hadn't I? We were in love and that was all that mattered. Richard didn't give a damn if I failed every single one of my O levels.

'I've only got two myself. History and Woodwork. I've got some CSEs, but nothing spectacular.'

He seemed genuinely unconcerned. But I was still indoctrinated with the belief that academic success mattered. I minded about Richard's. I told myself that it was because he hadn't gone to a very good school. If his family had been rich and posh and sent him to a public school then he'd have been taking his A levels this year. And he'd passed History, hadn't he, and that was quite a difficult subject.

'I think it was just a fluke more than anything else. I got on with the teacher okay.'

'But you're really interested in the past. You liked going round that country house, didn't you?'

145

'Yes, it was all right.'

'And remember you telling me about the day your parents took you to the Tower? You said you loved that day out.'

'Yes, but any kid likes that sort of thing.'

'No, they don't, most are bored stiff. Do you ever watch history programmes on television?'

'What, the schools things? No.'

'No, not schools programmes, but I bet you sometimes watch – I don't know, "Chronicle" or – what about those Michael Wood programmes on BBC 2?'

'I don't think I saw them. We're a bit conventional in our tastes in telly at our house – "Coronation Street," "The Two Ronnies," "Grandstand", that sort of thing. We don't watch BBC 2 much.'

'Exactly! I'm saying you'd probably enjoy the chance. Oh Richard, why don't you develop your interest in history a bit? Get a few books on the periods you like best. Join an evening class, maybe. Look, you can do A level history at classes, how about that?'

He was too polite to tell me straight out that he wasn't the slightest bit interested. I kept on nagging him, knowing it was pointless, but unable to give up. I badly wanted Richard to be clever, even if I now knew I wasn't. I wanted him to go to classes and get all sorts of qualifications and give up his printing job and go to university and be the sort of boy-friend I could boast about to all those idiots at school.

I was filled with a desperate longing to make him special. It was of imperative importance the day before my O level results were due. We had a special picnic tea at our house. Richard had given me some money and I'd bought French bread, cheese, greengages, a small strawberry gateau and a bottle of white wine. Richard brought a sharp knife and glasses and a corkscrew from home, and I had borrowed one of Mum's checked tablecloths. We sat cross-legged before our picnic and clinked our wineglasses together.

'Here's to us,' said Richard.

'Here's to the most perfect afternoon of the best summer of my life,' I said.

'I love you, Katy.'

'I love you, Richard.'

We sipped our wine slowly, and started on the food. I nibbled two greengages while Richard munched heartily at the bread and cheese.

'Eat, Katy. Please. You're getting so skinny.' He reached out and held my bony wrist. 'Look! A positive matchstick. You'll get ill. It's so daft working yourself up into this state about these boring old exams.'

'Don't talk about them!'

'Sorry, sorry. But honestly. You're acting as if everything's going to come to an end tomorrow.'

'Richard, please. Don't. Let's cut the cake. Give us the knife.'

'You can make a wish.'

'It's not a birthday cake.'

'You still get a wish though. I'll have one too. We'll cut the cake together.'

So we held on to the knife and cut through the strawberries and cream and sponge, our eyes shut. I tried to wish for eleven A's, but I knew it was pointless.

I didn't really want any cake, but I had a small piece to keep Richard happy. He ate two big slices, getting cream all round his lips. I leant over, put out my tongue and licked it up, and then we forgot about the picnic while we kissed.

The sky was going to fall tomorrow so it seemed ridiculous to worry about babies. But Richard remained resolutely sensible.

'Are you scared or something?'

'I'm thinking of you, not me,' said Richard, looking hurt. 'You've got your whole future in front of you.'

'Don't talk in clichés.'

'Don't patronise me.'

'I'm sorry. Richard, I really am – '

'You're just getting narked with me because you know I'm talking sense.'

'You're right. I suppose. Do you have to say narked?' But I said it gently as a joke and Richard smiled reluctantly.

'You're so bright, Katy. You're obviously going to go on to university and do really well for yourself, even though you've convinced yourself you've failed all these O levels. You don't want to muck up all your chances by having a baby.'

'I can't seem to get through to you. I *have* failed my exams. I'm not playing games, Richard. I don't know what I'm going to do.' I pulled crumbs off the French loaf, rolling little bits of bread between my fingers. I picked up the knife, stabbing idly at the loaf. Then I turned the knife round, pointing it towards my stomach.

'I could always commit hara-kiri, I suppose. Although it would be revoltingly messy. I don't want to die with six foot of smelly intestine exploding out of my stomach. How about cutting my wrists? That's still messy, but more decorous.' I held the knife against the prominent blue veins in my wrist. 'It shouldn't be that difficult. One really deep slash and they'd all start spouting like fountains.'

'Stop it,' said Richard, snatching the knife away from me. 'You shouldn't play around with knives.'

'Don't treat me the way you do Wendy.'

'Well, stop acting like a kid then.'

'Now who's being patronising? Hey, if you won't mingle flesh with me properly then how about mingling blood? Let's be blood brothers. One little nick from each of us. Come on, Richard, please.'

'All right then. But not your wrist! Thumbs. Although the knife's not disinfected or anything, and this is a germy old dump.'

'Stop being such an old woman. Jab your thumb then. You're scared now!'

But I was the one who found it extraordinarily difficult to stick the point of the knife into my own flesh. I tried again and again but my hand always lost its impetus at the last minute. Richard had to do it for me in the end.

It wasn't painful. We rubbed thumbs together hard and a spot of my blood mingled with his. We then sucked thumbs, giggling. It all seemed rather pointless. Perhaps sexual intercourse might have been equally disappointing.

Chapter 16

There was a clatter, a thrusting sound, and then a thump. The post had unmistakably arrived.

I stared at my empty plate. For once Mum had seen that it was pointless trying to make me eat. I could feel the three of them looking at me. I clutched the edge of the table and observed the pattern stamped on the cheap plate. A blue flower, a green flower, running alternately round and round. The blue flower had six petals, the green had four. I started to count the flowers themselves.

'Shall I go and get it?' said Nicola.

The flowers blurred and revolved, an indistinct turquoise roundabout. I had to look up.

'I'll go,' I said. Yes, they were all three staring at me. Nicola's mouth was open, her eyes screwed into slits. Mum's expression was identical, but blurred by excess fat. They looked comically grotesque, like a couple of jack-o-lanterns.

Dad had closed the shop for half an hour, an unprecedented move. His eyes were shining, his lips clamped, his hands clasped in front of his chest. He looked as if he was about to be given a wonderful present.

'Come on then, girl,' he said, his voice croaky with excitement.'

'It's going to be funny if it's just bills,' I said. 'I don't know for sure the results will be here today. The school couldn't guarantee it.'

'Well go and find out,' said Dad. 'Don't keep us here on tenterhooks.'

I stood up, still holding on to the table. The kitchen was revolving too. The lime green formica slid round to the ancient, blue stove, the stove shunted the kitchen cupboard sideways, the cupboard hurtled against the clothes rack of our damp, depressing underwear.

'Katherine! Watch out, she's going to faint,' Mum cried.

I shook my head, clinging for all I was worth. There were black blurs in front of my eyes but they went when I blinked, and the kitchen righted itself with an almighty lurch.

'I'm all right,' I said, and I walked unsteadily out of the kitchen and down the stairs.

There were two letters on the mat. I hardly glanced at one. The other was addressed to me, in my own handwriting. I held the envelope in both hands. I could tear it up there and then. Tear it into tiny pieces. My hands shook. I wanted to tear it up so badly. But that would only prolong the agony. They had to find out sooner or later.

'Well? Has it come? Katherine!' Dad called from the kitchen door. 'Bring the envelope up here.'

I did as I was commanded.

'Haven't you opened it? Come on, let's find out,' said Dad.

'I can't,' I whispered.

Dad chuckled. 'You're not going to find out standing there looking at the bally envelope. Open it!'

'Sit down, Katherine. Have a sip of tea, dear. You're as white as a sheet,' said Mum. 'Why not let Dad open it for you?'

'I'll open it myself,' I said, sitting down. 'Just give me a chance.'

I slid my finger under the flap of the envelope and tore it open an inch or so.

'Oh Kath, please!' Nicola begged, hugging herself and rocking backwards and forwards.

'I'll give her some encouragement,' said Dad, getting up and going to the cupboard. He stood on tiptoe to get to the top shelf, feeling behind old packets of prunes and barley and dried peas. He found a bottle. A big, green bottle of champagne. He lifted it down with a flourish.

'Champagne!' Mum gasped, and Nicola echoed her.

'Get a corkscrew, Mother, and the best glasses. Aha! Didn't spot where I'd hidden it, obviously.'

'A corkscrew and glasses?' Mum repeated. 'You don't mean we're going to drink it now?'

'Oh, we catch on quick in this household, don't we?' said Dad.

'But it's only just gone eight o'clock,' said Mum, looking at the kitchen clock for confirmation.

'I didn't ask you to tell me the time, I asked you to get the corkscrew,' Dad said. 'We're going to drink a toast to Katherine's success, and I don't care what the time is.'

'Champagne at breakfast!' Nicola muttered in awe.

'That's what all the nobs have. Champagne and orange juice. They call it Buck's fizz. So there you are,' said Dad, collecting corkscrew and glasses himself.

We'd never had champagne before. Dad had never even produced a bottle of wine. He bought a half bottle of Harvey's Bristol Cream sherry at Christmas and he drank a can of lager when he watched the Cup Final on television. Otherwise we were completely teetotal.

He had spent all that money on a bottle of champagne. He had such faith in my academic success that he was already struggling with the corkscrew, the bottle stuck between his legs.'

'You'd better wait a minute, Dad,' I said. 'Maybe there's nothing to celebrate.'

'Miss Gloom and Doom! Well, open that bally envelope,' said Dad, waving the corkscrew at me.

So I opened it right up and took out the slip of paper. I stared at it. For a moment none of it made any sense. Then I saw an A. Several A's. For one wonderful moment I thought everything was going to be all right. I'd got my A grades after all. I was still clever and Dad would still love me and no one would sneer at me at school.

But then I started reading the results properly line by line and I realised it wasn't all right. I hadn't got eleven A grades. I hadn't even passed all my O levels. I had failed Chemistry and Geography. I had only got a C in History and that was supposed to be one of my best subjects. I had a B in Physics, a B in Biology, a B in Greek. I had only five A grades, in French, Latin, Maths, English Language and English Literature.

I sat looking at the results, reading them through again, as if I seriously hoped that somehow they'd all turn into A grade passes.

'Well?' said Dad. 'Eleven A grades?'

But he had seen my expression and his voice was sharp.

I had to look up at him. The champagne bottle was still between his legs, protruding rudely. He clasped the neck of the bottle, his face sucked inwards like a skull with the intensity of his longing.

I shook my head at him, dying.

Nicola sniffed in agitation. Mum cleared her throat twice but didn't say anything.

Dad slowly removed the bottle and stood it on the table.

'What is it then?' he said, his voice heavy with disappointment. 'Did you get a B in something? Well, never mind dear. It's not the end of the world. Which subject was it? Katherine? Don't cry, dearie, look, we'll still have the champagne. You're not a little computer, we can't expect perfection every time. Of course you did it in your mocks, but never mind that now. It's not two B's, is it? Never mind, it doesn't really matter that much about the grade, just as long as you've passed all the bally things.'

'But I haven't, Dad,' I said. 'I've failed two. And I've got a C in History, and three B's.'

Dad stared at me as if I was mouthing obscenities.

'What are you on about?' he said weakly.

'I'm sorry, Dad. I'm sorry, I just couldn't. Oh Dad, please don't be cross with me,' I sobbed, putting my head down on the tablecloth.

I felt Nicola's hand reaching for mine and squeezing. I snatched my own hand away, sticking it between my knees.

'Pull yourself together, Katherine,' said Dad. He prodded me hard in the back. 'Come on, stop that slouching and snivelling. Give me those results.' He took them from me, drew his old, smeared reading-glasses from his cardigan pocket, and studied the paper.

'Dad – '

'Will you be quiet!' he snapped.

So we sat in silence while he read my results. Then he put the paper down on the table and sat still, his face a mask. Mum timidly reached out and looked at my results herself.

'Well, I don't see why there's all this upset,' she said. 'Maybe you haven't done quite as well as we expected, Katherine, but you've still done jolly well. Nine O levels! Goodness, that's far more than most girls get. And five A grades. I think that's really a result to be proud of. Well done! Come on then, Father. Let's open your lovely champagne.'

'Shut up,' said Dad.

He got up and walked straight out of the kitchen without looking at any of us. We heard him go down the stairs and out of the shop. The door banged.

'Oh dear,' said Mum. 'Oh well. Maybe he needs a little time to himself. But don't worry about it, Katherine. He's probably a bit disappointed but he'll soon get over it.'

'Stop it, Mum! Of course he won't get over it. Stop pretending everything's all right. He'll never forgive me and you know it.'

'Don't be silly, dear. There's no need to act like a Tragedy Queen. All this fuss over silly old O levels,' said Mum, laughing artificially. 'You've done very well really. I don't see what's so dreadful. You've done well enough to go to your precious university, when you've got your A levels. You're still going to have all the chances. You should be thankful.'

'I'd be thrilled to bits if I got nine O levels with five A grades,' said Nicola. 'You've done really well, Kath.'

'Yes, we all know *you'd* be thrilled. You're so thick it'll be a miracle if you pass even one O level. So stop being so patronising,' I shouted.

Nicola flinched as if I'd hit her. She went very red, trying not to cry.

'How can you be so unkind, Katherine?' Mum said. She was red too. 'I've just about had enough of this. I know you're in a state because your results aren't as good as you hoped but I'm not having you upsetting your sister like this. It's too bad of you. I don't think you've any idea how cruel you can be.'

'I didn't mean it,' I muttered.

'Yes you did,' Nicola wailed. 'I can't help not being clever like you. And I was trying to be *nice.*'

'Oh you poor little misunderstood creature,' I mocked. 'Sit on Mumsie's lap then and she'll stuff you with sweeties and make it all better.'

Mum heaved herself up and came and stood over me. She smelt strongly of sweat and talcum and fried food. I swivelled away from her.

'Don't you pull that face at me, as if I was dirt under your feet,' Mum hissed, and she got hold of me by the shoulders with her great hands. For the first time in my life I was really frightened of her. I felt the strength of her hands. I'd seen her wringing wet clothes, screwing showers of water from thick towels. I could feel the hatred in her hands, as if she wanted to twist my neck round and round like the wet washing.

'I've just about had enough of you. You act as if you're so hard done by and yet you're the lucky one of the family. How do you think Nicola feels? She's lived under your shadow all these years. She's always been compared with you and found wanting, poor little mite. Yet she's never ever resented it. She's always looked up to you, copied you, done every single thing for you. You've hit her and hurt her and taken her things and teased and tormented her, and yet she's put up with it all willingly because she thinks you're so wonderful. And what do you think it's been like for me? Put in my place by a pert little miss all the time. I've seen you smirking and raising your eyebrows and pulling silly faces. Don't you think I've got feelings, Katherine? Don't you know how it hurts when your own daughter acts as if you're some kind of joke?'

'Mum, don't! I didn't mean – it's not my fault – ' I whined.

She shook me hard.

'Maybe it wasn't your fault at first. I know just what a fool your father's made of you. Going on all the time about you being so gifted, practically encouraging you to look down on me, taking you everywhere with him and leaving us out, just talking to you about anything important. How do you think I've felt about that?' Mum shouted, spittle gleaming at the corners of her mouth.

I tried to focus on her face through the black blurs. The kitchen started revolving again and my brain seemed to tip upside down too. I had no idea she had such deep feelings. I hadn't thought she'd minded anything very much. I didn't want to know all this. It was so much easier to think of her as a great pink sofa who didn't mind being sat on.

'You shouldn't have let it happen then,' I said, wrenching

154

away from her. 'You should have stood up for yourself. You shouldn't have let Dad bully you.'

'You don't understand, do you? For all you're so clever you haven't got a clue. You don't know what it's like to love someone. Yes, Katherine, I love him. Don't you dare look so appalled! I love him even though he treats me like dirt.'

'Oh Mum, he doesn't mean to. Oh Mum, *I* love you,' Nicola moaned, trying to put her arms round her.

Mum patted her abstractedly, concentrating on me.

'You're the one he loves, Katherine, and you know it. You exploit the situation. You play up to him for all you're worth so don't play Little Miss Innocent with me.'

'Then you ought to be glad about my awful results,' I said, standing up. 'You saw what it did to him. He doesn't love me now. Didn't you see his face? So you've won.'

'How can you be so stupid? Of course I haven't won. You've made everything a hundred times worse, don't you see? He won't turn to me, he'll likely turn against me.'

'And me!' I said.

'He's made you his whole life, Katherine. It was so important to him that you did really well in your exams. He's never had the chance himself, and yet he's always been clever and known such a lot – '

'But why has he had to live his life through me? All right, I know he was poor, and he had to help in the shop when Grandad died so he couldn't stay on at school, I know all that, but why can't he do something now? What about the Open University? Or he could go to the Poly while you ran the shop. Why can't *he* do the studying and see what it's like?' I yelled.

'He did try once. Before you two were born. He went to night school,' said Mum. 'He tried ever so hard. He practically made himself ill, studying. But he couldn't keep up. It wasn't really his fault, he'd just got out of the habit of book learning. He had to give it up in the end, he was getting such headaches.'

'There! *I* get headaches. So why can't he sympathise with me a bit more? Why can't he understand? Why does he act like it's the end of the world because I haven't got all A grades?'

'Because it means so much to him. You mean so much. He's pinned all his hopes on you.'

155

'It's not my fault.'

'Yes it is.'

'What?' I couldn't believe she'd understood me properly. 'It's not my fault that I haven't done well in my exams.'

'Yes it is,' Mum repeated implacably, folding her arms over the great swell of her stomach.

'It's not! I tried so hard, I worked and worked, I practically had a breakdown. I'm just not clever enough now, I can't remember everything.'

'Don't give me that. You could remember it all for your mocks before you met this boy-friend of yours.'

'Boy-friend?'

'Don't pretend with me, Katherine. You've been messing around with this boy instead of concentrating on your school-work, that's why you've mucked up your O levels.'

'That's not true! I didn't even know Richard when I was taking my O levels. And anyway, how do you know?' I turned to Nicola, who shrank from me.

'You told her! You've told her all about Richard. You sneaking little cow!'

'I didn't tell Mum anything,' Nicola howled, and rushed across the kitchen, blundering into the vacuum cleaner as she went. She stubbed her toe badly and limped out of the room, sobbing.

Mum called after her but stayed with me.

'You're just never content with tormenting your sister,' she said. 'She didn't breath a word. She didn't have to. He introduced himself to me, remember?'

'Yes. Well. But what makes you think I've been seeing him since?'

'I don't think, I know. This business about you going to that nursery school! Your father might have swallowed that, but not me. I know what you've been up to. Messing about with him every day.'

'What do you mean, messing? Do you have to keep using that horrible expression?'

'Have you got a better name for it then, Miss Clever? Only I hope you've been clever enough not to get yourself into trouble. You know what I mean.'

'Stop it!' I shouted. 'Don't you dare turn it into something

156

sordid. We're in love with each other. You're trying to make me feel ashamed but I'm not, I'm not.'

'Then try telling all this to your father,' said Mum.

She'd won, and we both knew it. I picked up the results paper and the other envelope and went out of the kitchen. Nicola was in our bedroom. She'd got the fashion book beside her on her bed and was busy tearing up the paper people. Not just Mr Tremble. Pattie Pert fluttered to the floor, beheaded. Nicola tore off Miranda's arms and legs while I watched, and then started on Arabella.

'You are so pathetic,' I said scornfully, although inside I was quivering with sorrow and shame. 'You're just hurting yourself, not me. I don't like playing that stupid baby game. I'm thrilled that you're instigating all this paper carnage.'

Nicola stopped tearing. She looked round wildly. She saw my snowstorm, snatched it up, and hurled it with all her strength at the wall. We stared at it, holding our breath. The plastic couldn't shatter, but the dome buckled and came away from the base. The artificial snow blew into the air and then subsided for the last time, speckling the lino.

Mum shouted out from the kitchen, wondering about the thump. Nicola moaned and ran. I heard her thundering downstairs. I stood looking at my broken snowstorm. I could feel a pulse beating in my eyes. I left the bits where they were and went to lie on my bed. I looked at my results one more time and dropped them onto the floor. I was still holding the other envelope. I opened it.

It was a Good Luck card of a black cat attempting to cross its claws. I opened it up and found a message from 'Wendy'.

'Good luck with those results. I've got my fingers crossed for you too. I bet you've got top grades in all of them, but never mind if you haven't. From your very special friend, Wendy.'

I held the card to my chest as if it was a baby, stroking it. Why did the exam results matter so much when I had Richard? I loved him and that was all I was going to care about now. I whispered his name over and over again. It sounded as if Mum was sobbing in the kitchen.

I lay there for an eternity. Richard, Richard, Richard, Richard, Richard, Richard . . ..

Then I heard Dad shouting.

'Katherine! Katherine, come here! Come here at once, you bloody little liar!'

Richardrichardrichard . . ..

But it didn't work any more.

Chapter 17

I got up from my bed. I slotted my feet into my shoes and brushed my hair and rubbed at a small stain on my jeans while Dad shouted dementedly downstairs.

'Katherine!' Mum. I heard the creak of the stairs as she lumbered upwards. 'Katherine, your Dad wants you,' she panted.

'I'm coming.'

Mum opened the bedroom door and went on clinging to it, out of breath.

'He's beside himself,' she whispered. 'What are you going to say to him? Oh dear, there's been enough said already this morning to last a lifetime. Try not to make things worse, Katherine. You can sometimes calm him down. Try and get round him, please.'

I knew I was powerless now. I wanted to cower behind Mum's great bulk but my pride wouldn't let me. I swept past her and walked downstairs, although my legs were trembling so badly that my shoes made stuttering sounds on the stairs.

Dad was standing in the middle of the shop swaying with rage. His face was dark red, as if he'd burst his skin in his fury. His lips were flecked with white scum and his chest heaved rapidly. He had obviously been running. When he saw me he made a ferocious gobbling sound, his finger stabbing the air.

'You deceitful little cow!'

'Why are you calling me names?' I said, shivering.

'You know why!' Dad took several paces forward. 'Liar!' he barked right in my face. I knew he'd been about to shout, but I still couldn't stop myself jumping.

The shop bell pinged and Mrs Mackenzie came in. She was a regular customer, the only woman I knew who was the same size as Mum, give or take a stone or two. She beamed at us all, undid the last straining button on her raincoat, and gave a sigh of relief.

'That's better. It's so hot. I'm sweating in this mac, but they said it would rain later on. I'll have a *Woman's Weekly* dear, and shall I have a Yorkie or a Cadbury's fruit and nut for my elevenses?' she asked Dad.

'We're shut,' said Dad. 'You'll have to come back later.'

'Oh no!' said Mum worriedly from the back of the shop. 'Look dear, I'll serve Mrs Mackenzie. You go upstairs with Katherine while I look after the shop.'

Dad took no notice.

'We're shut,' he said, and he took hold of Mrs Mackenzie's arm and steered her none too gently towards the door. 'We're shut,' he repeated wildly, as he heaved Mrs Mackenzie out onto the street.

She couldn't catch her breath to protest until the door had slammed in her face. Dad bolted it with unnecessary fervour.

'You shouldn't have done that,' Mum said timidly. 'Not to Mrs Mackenzie. She can be ever so touchy. What ever will she think?'

'I don't give a damn what she thinks. I've got more important things on my mind than Mrs Fat Arse Mackenzie.'

Mum hissed with shock. I battled against hysteria.

'And you can take that grin off your face before I slap it off,' Dad said, turning back to me. His fists were clenched and in the air, as if he was actually about to let fly at me. 'I want an explanation for all these lies you've been telling me all bloody summer.'

'What lies? I don't know what you mean.'

'I've met the boy, dear, and he's really quite nice,' Mum gabbled. 'I'm sure it'll all blow over soon anyway.'

'Shut *up*, Mum!'

'What boy? What the hell are you talking about?' said Dad. 'I'm not talking about *boys*. I've just been to see Mrs Philpotts.'

'You haven't!' I said, taken aback.

'Oh yes I have. *I* don't tell lies.'

'But how could you? She's not at school.'

'I didn't see her at the school, did I? I looked her up in the phone book and went to see her at her home. I was all set to give her a piece of my mind.'

160

'Oh, you shouldn't have,' said Mum. 'What ever did she think?'

'She thought I was a concerned parent, wondering why the hell my brilliant daughter has ended up with such indifferent exam results. I said it just wasn't good enough, that it was obvious there'd been some kind of mistake, because Katherine got eleven A grades in her mocks. I said I wanted an explanation from the school as to why she's suddenly doing so badly. I said that it was about time they started concentrating more on academic success than on damn daft nursery school projects.' He emphasised the last three words with relish.

He paused a moment, a master of timing. I waited helplessly.

'Mrs Philpotts didn't seem to know what I meant so I filled her in on what you'd been doing all summer, Katherine. And then Mrs Philpotts told me that there was obviously some misunderstanding. She doesn't *know* about any nursery school project. She says you were only at the bally school a *week*. And then she added that you *couldn't* have been going there all this time because it closes for the summer holidays just like an ordinary school. I just stood there with my mouth open. I couldn't credit it. You've been lying to me all this time. Not just one lie, one day. You've been telling me a whole tissue of lies this entire summer. So what have you been doing with yourself, Katherine Petworthy? And you'd better tell me the truth or by God, I'll beat it out of you.'

'I've been seeing my boy-friend,' I said boldly.

I enjoyed saying it and seeing him reel. It would have come out anyway. Sooner or later he would have returned to Mum's remark and worried the truth out of her.

'What do you mean, boy-friend?' Dad said, looking utterly disgusted, as if I'd suddenly sprouted great spots all over my face. 'What boy-friend? What do you mean? You're fifteen years old. You're still a little girl!'

'I said, dear, I've met the boy, and he was very polite and charming. He seems very well brought up. He's not a yobby sort at all,' Mum twittered.

Her words registered this time. Dad's head swivelled. 'You're saying you knew Katherine was seeing some boy and you did nothing about it?' Dad said. 'So it's all your fault, is it?'

161

Silence roared in the room. It was my chance. Mum started little whimpering noises of distress.

'I – I didn't really – I mean, I didn't see – Oh, I'm sorry.'

'You fat fool,' said Dad.

She stared at him and then her face dissolved. Her whole body shook as she wept. I'd heard Dad abuse her often but he'd never once referred to her weight in the past. Somehow those three short syllables seemed the most insulting words in the world.

I stared at both my parents and felt my old allegiance evaporating. Righteous anger on Mum's behalf overcame my own fear and self pity.

'Don't you dare call her that!' I shouted, and I leapt forward and attacked my father, clawing at his face ineffectually with my bitten finger-nails. 'You hateful pig, you always have to turn on her and make it all her fault, but it isn't, it isn't. And it isn't my fault either. I tried so hard to do well in my O levels, I worked so much, you *know* I did. But I couldn't do it this time, I couldn't remember everything. I just wasn't clever enough, can't you see that? It's *your* fault. You've kept on and on at me, trying to turn me into a child genius, but I'm not, I'm not, you *pig.*'

I expected him to turn on me and give me the threatened beating. But he didn't even try to catch hold of my hands and stop me. He just stood there, trying to protect his face, almost cowering from me. I started running out of energy and didn't know what to do. I could hear my voice screaming hysterically but it seemed utterly out of my control. My fingers lost contact with his face and waved wildly in the air. At last I stepped back and ran for the door. I unbolted it and shot out into the sunshine.

Mrs Mackenzie and two supporters were standing outside the shop eavesdropping. They made little oohing noises as I rushed out. I ran past them and kept on running until I was round the corner. I leant against a wall, gasping for breath. I squeezed my eyes shut, wishing I could close my ears too and blank out the noise of the street. If only I could will myself into a deep sleep and then wake up in bed and find that this was all a nightmare. But it was real. It was far worse than I'd even imagined. The sky was pressing down on my head.

162

I had my hand up over my eyes. Tears trickled under my closed eyelids and leaked onto my hand. Someone stopped beside me and touched my shoulder gently.

'What's the matter, dear? Can I help?'

I shook my head blindly.

'You're not in pain, are you? You seem so upset. There's a café up the road, do you want to come and have a sit down there?'

I opened the sore cracks of my eyes. A motherly, middle-aged woman was looking at me worriedly. Her hair was permed into fluffy baby curls and her spotted dress smelt faintly of Comfort. She wasn't wearing tights and her pale, shaved legs looked as smooth and shiny as soap. She seemed so kind and clean and soft and sensible. If only she was my mother, and I had an ordinary, gentle father to match. I had an insane desire to throw my arms round her neck and beg her to look after me, but I shook my head at her, grunted an apology, and started running again.

I couldn't get my breath and my throat ached and I had a stitch in my side and my feet burned as they stubbed the pavement. I couldn't go on running, but if I stopped then someone else would come along and ask me questions. I ended up running to our house because I needed somewhere to hide, but when I got there I felt lonelier than ever.

I lay down on the rug and sniffed at an edge of the wool as if it was a cuddle blanket, rubbing it against my damp nose. I reminded myself of Nicola and I shook my head and mumbled nononono to distract myself, too guilty to think about what I'd said to my sister. I chanted Richard's name instead and felt such a wave of longing for him that I started groaning. I snuffled into the rug, imagining it smelt faintly of his talcum powder. I pulled the wool tightly round me, trying to pretend that it was Richard's arms holding me, but the rug's embrace was empty and ineffectual. I wanted the real Richard. Pretending wasn't enough.

I was supposed to be meeting him at two o'clock but I couldn't wait. I knew where he lived although I'd never been to his house. He'd be there on his own. His mother worked until one o'clock and whiny little Wendy spent every morning with her Auntie so that Richard had peace to sleep after his night-shift.

I thought of him lying in his bed and the only thing I wanted in the whole world was to creep in beside him and go to sleep with his arms round me. So I unwound the rug and got up off the floor and left our house. I knew I'd probably never be able to go back. I went into every room except the fearful lavatory, pretending it was clean and comfortable and fully furnished, but as I climbed carefully down the rotting staircase the house reverted to its original squalor and I couldn't imagine it any other way. It was a relief to squeeze out of the broken window and stand in the unkempt garden, weeds worrying my ankles. I waded through the greenery and then started running again, desperate to get to Richard.

I thought I knew how to get to the road where he lived, but it was part of a large nineteen-thirties estate and each road looked identical. I ran up and down Sycamore Road and Ash Crescent and Beech Avenue, unable to locate Maple Lane. There were no trees at all, in spite of the woody names. The pavements were neatly bare. Even the gardens looked artificial, the plants clipped like poodles.

I stopped a woman with a toddler and asked her the way to Maple Lane. She gave me detailed directions while her little girl nibbled at a King Cone, frowning. As I thanked the mother the little girl announced, 'She's been crying, her eyes are all red. That big girl's been crying, Mum! Did you see, that big girl, she'd been *crying.*'

The big girl started crying again when she realised she'd forgotten half the directions and still had no idea how to find Maple Lane, but after I'd wandered miserably round the maze for a further ten minutes it suddenly materialised in front of me.

Number 56 didn't have a proper garden any more. It had been paved in pink and green squares, but there were little tubs of petunias at either side of the front door. The living-room curtains were rose Dralon, with pink netting to match. I looked upwards. There were frilly ruched curtains and a crinoline lady at one bedroom window, and a row of yellowing dolls at the other. Richard's room must be at the back.

I walked up the checkered path, keeping off the cracks.

164

Pink, green, pink, green, pink to the front door. It was painted as purple as the petunias. No wonder Richard didn't have a subtle sense of colour. But I didn't care about any of Richard's so-called faults. Just so long as he held me in his arms and loved me he could wink and talk slang and shave his hair right to his scalp and I wouldn't care.

I rang the bell timidly. I heard it chiming inside but nothing happened. I rang again, leaving my finger on the bell. I waited, straining for the sound of footsteps, but the house was silent. I opened the letter-box and peered into the hall. I saw pink carpet, a chopper bike leaning against the bannisters, scattered Lego bricks, and one of Richard's sweaters curled up on the stairs like a cat.

'Richard?' I called through the letter-box. My voice was a croaky whisper. I cleared my throat and tried again, louder. But still nothing happened. The house was so quiet I could hear a clock ticking somewhere and the steady hum of a fridge. I shouted again and then straightened up despairingly. How could he sleep when I was bellowing his name? Perhaps he wasn't even in. Perhaps he'd got up early and gone out somewhere. Oh God, perhaps he'd gone to find me to see how I'd done in my exams.

I imagined the reception he'd get if he tried to come into the shop. I started hammering at the letter-box. When I stopped at last I thought I heard something upstairs. I rattled and banged again and then I heard someone fumbling with the door. It opened – and there was Richard, standing blinking and bewildered in his pyjamas. Not the blue and white striped sort I'd fondly imagined – slippery, mustard coloured bri-nylon. But I didn't care, I didn't care.

'Oh Richard, I'm sorry, but I just had to see you. Please don't be cross with me,' I sobbed.

'Come here,' he said, and he pulled me in and shut the door. He held me close against his chest and I clung to him. He smelt stale, of bedclothes and unbrushed teeth, but I snuffled into him, loving his smell, loving him.

He let me cry for a couple of minutes, and then he gently held me away from him.

'Come on. We'll make a cup of tea and then you can tell me all about it.'

165

I didn't want to sit down at a breakfast table. I wanted to curl up with him in his bed and hide there for ever, but I followed him into the kitchen. He put the kettle on, yawned and covered his mouth apologetically, although he couldn't help glancing at the clock. It was a quarter to eleven.

'What time did you get to bed?'

'About half past seven. No, later, I played with Wendy for a bit first.'

'Oh Richard, I'm sorry. Look, go back to bed.'

'I'm fine now,' said Richard, stretching and then scratching his chest. 'I don't need much sleep.' He saw me watching him scratching and stopped. 'Sorry.'

'It's me that should keep saying sorry. But I just needed to see you so badly. I couldn't wait till this afternoon.'

He smiled as I found cups and saucers, and I realised that he loved me needing him.

'Thank you for your card. It was very sweet of you,' I said.

'Well? Are you going to keep me in suspense?'

I chewed at my lip, growing hot. I realised just how many people I'd have to tell. If it was awful admitting my failure to Richard what was it going to be like telling the girls at school?

'I – I mucked them up. Most of them, anyway,' I mumbled.

I watched him carefully. He poured boiling water into the teapot and stirred it efficiently. His face betrayed nothing but concentration on making the tea. Then he put the spoon down and faced me properly. He looked sorry for me, but not overwhelmingly so, and I relaxed a little.

'Did you fail them all?'

'Of course not! I got A's in five of them.'

Richard looked baffled.

'Then what on earth are you in such a state about?'

'But I did fail two, Chemistry and Geography. And I only got a C for History, that's awful.'

'So how many have you actually passed?'

'Nine.'

'Nine! But that's marvellous! I can't understand you. You've passed nine O levels and you've got this A grade you wanted in five of them! Isn't that good enough? I mean, you'll be able to go into the sixth form and then go on to university, won't you?'

166

'I suppose so.'

'Then why on earth aren't you thrilled? You told me before you were utterly convinced you'd failed the lot.'

'Yes, but – '

I didn't know how to explain to Richard. It might have been easier if I had failed every single subject. At least that would have been sensational, flamboyant, dramatic. My results were galling because they were so nearly good, brighter than average but not really outstanding. They weren't special in any way.

'What did your Dad say?' Richard asked, pouring us both tea. He held out a chair for me and I sat down heavily. Dad. At least that was dramatic.

'He was appalled. There was a terrible row. He went storming off to see my headmistress of all people and he found out from her that I haven't been going to the nursery school all this time.'

'Oh God.'

'And he found out about us, Richard. He – he threatened to beat me. It was so awful. He closed the shop up and shouted and shouted at me and then we had this terrible fight – '

Richard put his cup down and held on to my hand.

'A real fight? You mean he hit you?'

'Well, sort of – and I tried to claw his face and – oh, it was horrible,' I said, crying.

Richard pulled me onto his lap.

'You poor little girl,' he said fiercely. 'How dare he hit you. Shall I go and punch him in the nose for you?'

I started giggling through my tears. I knew perfectly well I was distorting what had happened but I badly wanted Richard's sympathy.

'I don't know what I'm going to do, Richard. I'm so scared of him. And my mother's turned on me too. They think it's all my fault that I've not done well in my exams. I can't face the thought of going back there. I know Dad will never ever forgive me.'

'You don't have to go back there,' said Richard, rocking me. 'You can stay here, Katy. You can stay as long as you like. I'll look after you, don't worry.'

Chapter 18

We ended up in bed together after all. It was supposed to be just for a cuddle. I asked Richard in a tiny baby voice and he lifted me in his arms and carried me upstairs, although it was a struggle by the time he got to the top. His chest rose and fell dramatically and he grew red in the face, but he made it to his room and tipped me gently onto his bed.

I was disappointed by his bedroom. It didn't seem to have any Richard flavour at all. It had blue patterned wallpaper, blue and white checked curtains, and blue cord carpet (all slightly differing shades of blue). The furniture was unpainted whitewood: a wardrobe, a chest of drawers and a little locker beside his bed. There were a few posters and cuttings pinned up on the wall but they were crumpled at the edges, football and pop stars that were at their peak two or three years ago. Two slightly tarnished cups and a plastic shield were scattered on the top of the chest of drawers, but they were just school sports trophies. A shiny china carthorse, a mottled leaping dolphin and several little copper vases of plastic flowers littered the window sill but they surely weren't Richard's personal possessions.

'Where are all your things?' I asked, as Richard lay on top of his narrow divan bed beside me.

'What things?'

'Your toys, for a start. Old teddies and dinky cars and train sets, the special things too precious to throw away.'

'I cleared all that sort of junk out years ago.'

'What, all of it? Well, what about old drawings, exercise books full of train and car numbers, marbles, birds' eggs, whatever you collected?'

'I didn't collect anything.'

'Oh Richard! You *must* have. What's in the chest of drawers? Any interesting bits and pieces?'

'Pants, vests, socks, sweaters, T-shirts, shirts,' he said, pointing to each drawer. 'All clean, all reasonably tidy, but not what you'd call interesting.'

'What about in your locker?'

'There's nothing much in there, just junk,' said Richard, but his voice was wary.

I wriggled over him and pulled the locker open before he could stop me.

'Aha!' I said triumphantly, rummaging through the muddle.

'Come out of there, nosy,' said Richard. 'Look, there's nothing there. Maybe a few sweaty socks, bits of rubbish – I just use it as a glory hole. Leave it alone. Come and wriggle over me again, I liked that.'

But I wouldn't take any notice of him. I was too busy ferreting through the sordid little sock balls and grubby hand-kerchieves for something interesting. There were several books, *Tom Sawyer*, *Kidnapped*, *David Copperfield*, even *Moby Dick*. Various aunties and grannies had written fond birthday and Christmas messages on the flyleaves. All the presents were in pristine condition, obviously unread. But there were a few paperbacks too, and they were all well thumbed. They weren't my taste particularly, mostly thrillers and war books, but at least Richard read something.

'What are you going through all those for?'

'Let me look, please.'

'You are a weird girl.'

'I know, it's all part of my charm,' I said, pulling out the things at the back of the locker.

I was thrilled when I found an old stamp album. There weren't many stamps stuck in, but that didn't matter. I found he'd done little cartoon drawings in the squares of the back pages, and that was even better. I pored over the tiny pinmen pictures.

'I don't get you,' said Richard. 'Look at what they're saying.' He pointed to the uneven printing. '"I'll biff you one. I'll bash you up. Get your dirty mitts off me". It's all the sort of words that make you do your nut.'

'Don't use that expression! It's different here. It's appropri-ate. And it's lovely, you making up your own cartoons when

169

you were a little boy. Don't you see, I want to find out all about you. You never tell me anything.'

I abandoned the album and found an old puppet with its strings horribly tangled. It was an odd, white horse with soulful eyes.

'Who's this?'

'Oh. That's Muffin. The Mule. It used to be on telly when my Mum was a little girl. It was her Muffin and she kept him and my brother had him and then he was passed on to me.'

'How lovely. So you kept him because he's special?'

'No, I kept him because I got the strings all tangled up and I knew Mum would go spare if she found out so I shoved him right to the back of my locker and he's been there ever since.'

'Oh Richard! You are sweet.'

'Anyway, put him back now. And all the other junk. Come on, Katy, come and have your cuddle.'

But there was still something else right at the back of the locker, hidden in a brown paper bag.

'What are you doing? Give that here! Leave it *alone!*'

But I'd shaken several magazines out of the paper bag. Sexy magazines. I opened one up at the centre pages.

'Ugh!'

'Yes. Well. You shouldn't go nosing in other people's things. Put them back in the bag.'

'Honestly! Where did you get them, Richard? You didn't buy them?'

'I got them from this bloke at work.'

'What for?'

'I don't know. Curiosity, I suppose. They're just filth. I wouldn't keep them, but I don't want my Mum to find them in the dustbin.'

'All the same, they look very well thumbed to me,' I said, giggling.

'Put those stupid magazines down.' He pulled them out of my hand, we struggled and wrestled, and then, of course, we kissed.

'I do love you, Katy,' he whispered, his head buried in my neck.

'I love you.' I put my arms round him, clinging. 'Oh Richard, if only we could stay here for ever and ever. If only I didn't

170

have to go home, if only I didn't have to go to school ever again.'

'I told you, you can stay,' said Richard seriously.

He sat up and fiddled with the piece of string round my neck on which I wore his little silver ring. He slipped it off and then put it on the third finger of my left hand.

'Will you marry me?' he whispered.

I was very moved, although I also felt a terrible urge to giggle.

I nodded, not trusting my voice.

'I'll get you a proper ring later on, as soon as I've got enough money saved. You can stay here, Katy. I don't think Mum would let us share my room but you could easily go in with Wendy. She's got bunk beds so that's no problem. And you don't have to go back to school either, not if you really don't want to.'

'I could work in a jeans shop, like Jeanette,' I said.

'But I don't think you'd like it much. You'd get ever so bored, wouldn't you? That's the trouble, you're not going to get a good job, not even with your O levels. Perhaps you ought to stick it out at school for another two years and – '

'I'm not going to sit another exam in my whole life,' I said fiercely. 'I think it would be lovely working in a shop and earning lots of money. Think of the clothes I could buy! Real, fashionable shop clothes, not these awful things my Mum makes.' But I didn't want to think about Mum. I saw her big face blotchy with tears and I shook my head vigorously to blur her.

'What on earth are you doing?'

'Just having one of my funny turns. Don't take any notice. Give me a big kiss, come on. Divert me.'

We were both diverted, totally absorbed in each other in the hot, dark world of Richard's bed. Then we curled up together properly under the covers, although it was rather a squash. It was lovely sitting on Richard's knees with his arms round me, keeping me safe. He stroked me gently with his hands, commenting on my sharp little elbows and the exaggerated keyboard of my ribs, telling me that his Mum would soon fatten me up, but his voice gradually slurred and his hands became heavier and I realised he was asleep.

171

I knew he was exhausted. He had a perfect right to sleep but I felt as if he'd abandoned me. I tried to sleep myself but when I closed my eyes I saw the piece of paper with my O level results. My ears were muffled with bedclothes but I kept hearing Dad's shouting, Mum's sobbing. Anyway, what if I got to sleep and then didn't wake up in time for Richard's mother when she came home at half past one? It would be dreadful if she found me tucked up in bed with her son.

So I carefully unclasped Richard's arms and slid out of bed. I crept out of his room and along the landing to the bathroom. The bath and basin and lavatory were an alarming shade of maroon, as if someone had severed several arteries and bled everywhere. I opened the medicine cabinet and found several razors. I held a rusting Gillette Techmatic to my wrist experimentally, but I wasn't serious. I put it away and poked for a while amongst the Golden Eye ointment and Quinoderm and Head and Shoulders shampoo, but there was nothing remotely interesting. I didn't like looking at my face in the cabinet mirror. I wanted to look romantically pale and grief stricken but my face was still puffy with tears, I had a spot coming on my nose, and my hair was exploding everywhere. I smelt stale too, of sweat and sex.

I borrowed someone's powder pink flannel, soaped myself liberally with expensive Pink Lilac, and then dared borrow a toothbrush too. I wished I could scour the inside of my head as well as the inside of my mouth.

When I was finished in the bathroom I had a further prowl upstairs. I found another bedroom that presumably belonged to Richard's brother Mick, the owner of the horrible cream jacket. He had bought his share of sex magazines too, but he didn't share Richard's shame. Girls with great drooping bosoms were stuck with blobs of bluetack to the wallpaper. He'd put the bluetack under their prominent nipples to give a three-dimensional effect. I was sure I was going to hate Mick.

Wendy's room at the front of the house was more or less as I'd expected, although I was surprised by the vast number of her toys. She had a proper matching suite of bedroom furniture, but only half size, specially for a small girl. I sat down on the pink padded stool in front of her little dressing-table and touched her brush and comb set, her Pretty Peach talcum and skin perfume, her jewellery box. I opened it up and a tiny plastic ballet dancer started revolving to a tinkling distortion of the 'Sugar Plum Fairy'. Wendy had several bits of plastic rubbish, the bracelets and rings they give away free in girls' comics, but she had some real pieces too. A Mickey Mouse wrist-watch, a small gold locket, a silver chain with an elaborate silver charm of the old woman who lived in a shoe. I flicked the catch so that the lid of the little silver boot lifted to show all the naughty children and the old woman inside.

Inevitably I thought how Nicola and I would have liked to have had real jewellery, real perfume, real matching furniture, when we were Wendy's age. Nicola would want all this even now, when she was so tall she'd tower over the dressing-table and break the little stool if she sat on it. Nicola. Oh God, I couldn't think about her either.

I rushed out of Wendy's room and peeped inside Richard's parents' bedroom. It was pink and white like Wendy's, but a grown-up version, the furniture embellished with twiddly bits of gilt. *Cherry Ripe* simpered on the wall. The bed was covered with pink and white puckered silk. A pair of pink fluffy mules were propped neatly side by side on a sheepskin rug. I tried putting one on. She had much bigger feet than me.

I opened up her wardrobe. I expected her clothes to be bright and garish like her house but they were rather subdued, fawns and greys and insipid blues. I shut the door on them and went to the dressing-table. It was like a counter at Boots. I dabbed on a few perfumes and tried an eye-shadow, taking great care not to spill. It was all so clean even though it was so crowded, everything beautifully dusted and wiped and polished to a high shine. She must spend every afternoon genuflecting with a duster at her own little altar. I knew I wasn't going to like her either.

I went back to Richard. He was still fast asleep on his back, one hand up by his face, the fingers curled slightly. He looked so relaxed and defenceless. It seemed odd that he could go on sleeping so peacefully with me peering at him.

I'd heard of lovers staying awake all night to watch the sleeping features of the beloved. It was a very romantic concept – but after I'd spent five minutes contemplating Richard I was very bored.

I opened his locker again and looked at the stamp album, but the little cartoons were not really very pleasing. They were crudely drawn and derivative. I tried *Moby Dick* but after the first paragraph the words started waving up and down and I floated helplessly, unable to grasp any shred of sense or meaning. I had an A grade in English Literature but it was no help. I was just an articulate imposter. I had read and studied my set books and practised a whole sequence of essays and had managed to get that A grade by writing like an automaton. I had no real aptitude or intelligence at all. There was no point in going back to school. I might bluff for a bit but they'd soon find me out. Miss Hyde had known the last time I'd been to tea with her. The teachers would be sad and sorrowful, the girls bitchily delighted. I wouldn't be able to stand the humiliation.

I closed *Moby Dick* with a snap and returned it to the locker. I would live here with Richard and sell jeans and . . . and that was all.

I looked at him again, trying to summon up a passionate love for him. His mouth was slightly open, his hair childishly ruffled, his head at an awkward angle on the pillow so that it emphasised his heavy jowls.

I woke him at one. I did it gently, putting one hand on his arm and whispering his name. He opened his eyes at once and looked at me blankly, as if he had no idea who I was. I wanted to weep with disappointment. I had hoped he'd wake with a smile, whispering my name, holding out his arms to me. He *did* smile after a few seconds, but it was too late. And it wasn't a genuine smile. He looked anxiously at the clock and then sprang from his bed. I knew he was dreading his mother coming home.

When he had washed and dressed we went downstairs and sat in the lounge, waiting. I fidgeted on the fat foam cushions of the sofa, holding my own hands, while Richard prowled up and down the wildly patterned carpet, telling me that I mustn't worry, that everything would be all right, that his mother wouldn't mind putting me up at all, that she would be thrilled to meet me at last.

Then we heard the back door open and Wendy chattering.

'Richard's up!' she said, and I remembered the cups of tea we'd left unwashed in the kitchen.

174

'Richard?'

I saw Richard swallow, his chin tucking into his neck in his panic.

'I – we're in here, Mum.'

Wendy came running, and a moment after her Mrs Cole came into her lounge. She was younger than I'd expected, with short, blonde hair and a good figure, although she was tall and she had a big bottom. She wore a pale blue blouse, matching trousers with creases that looked as if they'd cut her legs, and a grey sleeveless tunic thing that she obviously wore to keep her bottom covered at the back. I'd wanted her to be a bit tarty, a bit common, a bit past-it, so that I needn't feel quite so afraid of her, but there was very little I could sneer at. Her hair might have been helped with a blonde rinse or two, but it wasn't crudely platinum, and her make up was subtle.

'It's Katy, Mum!' said Wendy.

'So I see,' she said. She smiled at me and held out her hand.

I stood awkwardly and we shook hands. My palm was moist with sweat, hers was cool and clean. I was surprised she didn't wipe her hand afterwards on her tunic.

'Hello, Katy. How nice to meet you. Richard's told us a lot about you,' she said pleasantly. 'Well now, shall we all have a spot of lunch? I'm afraid it won't be anything too elaborate. You should have told me you were inviting Katy round,' she said, glancing at Richard.

He reddened uneasily. He looked strangely young standing there in front of his mother, almost a little boy.

Chapter 19

Lunch seemed exceptionally elaborate to me. We had tomato soup and warmed white rolls, then toasted cheese sandwiches made in one of those special machines, and a side salad to go with them. Mum's salad meant soggy lettuce. Mrs Cole's salad was a meal in itself: tomatoes cut into pretty patterns, shredded carrot, raisins, sweetcorn, apple chunks and tiny sprigs of lettuce that had been washed dried and thoroughly pampered. Then she produced scoops of vanilla ice-cream decorated with crescents of tinned peach and doused in bright red sauce.

I ate politely but I had to give up half-way through my pudding. It was much too sweet but it left an acrid aftertaste in my mouth. It reminded me of Mrs Cole.

She was being ultra charming to me, asking me a shower of silly questions like which magazines did I buy (she had *Woman* and *Woman's Own* every week and she sometimes treated herself to *Cosmopolitan* too although it could be a bit crude at times) and which telly programmes did I like best (she liked a nice historical serial, she loved the costumes) and where had I been for my holiday this year (she was thinking about going abroad next year, the thought of flying had always held her back before but that was silly, wasn't it, and she couldn't help going green with envy listening to the girls at her salon going on about Benidorm and Rimini and Llorret, it was time they branched out a bit, especially now Wendy was growing up). Eventually her questions drizzled and stopped, and she concentrated on Wendy instead, telling her to eat up nicely and stop picking, while Wendy whined and showed off.

Richard and I said very little. Even his appetite seemed affected. Mrs Cole shook her head sadly when he left half his sandwich.

'It's being on nights. You know I go off my food,' Richard said hurriedly.

'First I've heard of it,' said Mrs Cole. She watched him yawn. 'You shouldn't have got up so early, my lad. You look worn out.'

I felt myself reddening.

'I'm fine,' said Richard.

'I'm sorry,' I muttered. 'I shouldn't have come round, but – '

I waited, unable to continue. I hoped Richard would say it for me and ask if I could stay, but he seemed as awkward as myself. He still hadn't asked his mother when we went to do the washing-up together.

'Shall I ask her?' I whispered.

'No! I'll do it. But let's wait for an opportune moment, eh?'

'What if there isn't one? Richard, she's not daft, she can sense something's up. Wouldn't it be better to ask her straight out?'

'Leave it for a bit. I'll make her a cup of tea and then while she's watching the television I'll bring the subject up.'

'She's not going to want me to stay though, is she?'

'Yes, of course she is. She's just got to be handled right. She can be a bit dodgy sometimes like all women, but I'm good at getting round her.'

'But I don't want you to have to get round her. You made out she wouldn't mind a bit, that we'd just ask and she'd say yes and that would be it.'

'Well, that's the way it will be. I'm just giving the two of you a chance to get to know each other, that's all. You're getting on really well, it's great.'

'Are you mad? She doesn't like me a bit.'

'Yes, she does. She's being ever so nice.'

'But it's all false and horrible. Underneath she's wondering what on earth you see in me and why am I here disrupting your family routine. And she keeps looking at my awful hair. Why does she have to be a hairdresser of all things? I hate hairdressers.'

'Don't be silly,' said Richard. 'You don't hate my Mum.'

I did hate her, but I didn't dare admit it. I finished the washing-up in silence and dried my hands, wincing. I'd been picking my hangnails all day and they were bleeding.

'Look at your hands! You ought to wear rubber gloves,' said Richard.

'I wouldn't be seen dead in rubber gloves,' I said. 'I can't stick people who wear rubber gloves and Rainmates and those fold-up royal blue anoraks and act as if a bit of water would wash them all away.'

Richard didn't reply. When he hung up the towel I saw his mother's bright pink rubber gloves waving at me from the rack.

When we went back to the lounge Wendy pounced on Richard, wanting him to play with her. Richard moaned and told her to leave him alone and Wendy started pouting, near to tears.

'She hasn't seen much of you recently, Richard,' said Mrs Cole. 'You're nearly always either sleeping or out.' Her eyes flickered in my direction. 'One little game wouldn't hurt, would it?'

One little game led to one more and one more. Richard tried to get me to join in too, but Wendy didn't want that.

'I'll get her Madeleine to look at, okay?' she said. 'You like dolls, don't you, Katy?'

She brought me Madeleine and a legless Amanda Jane baby and a pink knitted doll with cross-eyes and unravelled wool plaits and finally she brought me a monstrous head with a vacant expression and no body at all. Wendy arranged them in my lap.

I sat surrounded by Wendy's unattractive progeny, trapped. If Mrs Cole hadn't been there I might have tried to make them all real. The head had infinite possibilities. I'd soon have Wendy cowering. But Mrs Cole *was* there, sitting in a large armchair in front of the television, her long, trousered legs propped up on a square of fur fabric that Wendy called a pouffe. She called it that many times, giggling. Mrs Cole sighed and told her not to be silly. She was watching an afternoon repeat of some romantic series that she obviously enjoyed. Whenever the background violins grew shrill with emotion she wriggled and her trousered legs rasped. She'd kicked off her pink fluffy slippers. She was wearing bright tan tights underneath her trousers. I stared at her feet. They didn't seem to smell at all – I'd seen the foot deodorant spray in the bathroom – but they were very long and large and all her toes were misshapen, curling under like claws.

178

She looked up when the commercial break began and caught me staring.

'Hairdressing's very hard on the feet, dear,' she said, bending over and rubbing her toes. 'They're giving me gyp right this minute. Richard, be a love.'

To my surprise Richard shuffled over to his mother and knelt at her feet. He started massaging one foot with smooth even strokes. Mrs Cole sighed and put her head back.

'Bliss!' she murmured.

I was revolted. I couldn't bear to watch Richard's hands on her horrible feet. Mrs Cole closed her eyes and smiled. I wanted to slap his hands away. What was the matter with him? Why did he let these two frightful females boss him about? Couldn't he see that it diminished him as a man? But he wasn't a man yet. He was just a big soft silly boy.

We sat it out grimly all afternoon. When 'Grange Hill' started on the television Wendy decided she didn't want to play any more, but she still wouldn't relinquish her hold on her brother. She climbed up on Richard's lap and lolled there triumphantly, looking ridiculous.

'I can't bear that programme. The way those kids behave!' said Mrs Cole. 'Well. I suppose I'd better go and see about supper. Get it on at any rate. Dad and Michael will be home soon.'

There was a little pause as she sighed and stood up.

'Katy, are you staying to supper?' she said.

I looked at Richard in agony.

'You don't mind, do you, Mum?' he said.

'Well, no, of course I don't mind.'

I cleared my throat.

'Mrs Cole, I – this sounds awful but – well, Richard said – ' I didn't have the courage to come straight out with it. I made Richard do it after all.

'Would it be all right if Katy stayed the night, Mum?'

Mrs Cole frowned and folded her arms.

'No Richard, she can't.' She turned to me. 'I'm sorry, dear, but we haven't got a spare bedroom.'

'She could sleep in the bunk bed in Wendy's room. Please say yes. Katy won't be any bother.'

'Richard, it's all right,' I said. 'I'll go home now.'

'But you can't. I'm not having your father frightening you. You've got to stay here. Look, you can have my room because I'll be out doing my night-shift.'

'Don't be silly, Richard. We're not fiddling about changing sheets tonight and then first thing in the morning.'

'For God's sake, Mum, can't we use the same sheets? I don't see why you're being so awkward about it. Babs stays here with Mick whenever she wants and no one makes a big fuss.'

'That's different. They're engaged.'

'Well, so are Katy and I,' said Richard desperately.

'What did you say?' said Mrs Cole.

'Are you and Katy *engaged*?' Wendy shrieked. 'Where's her ring then? Is it the ring I chose? Is it that one, Richard?'

'Wendy, be quiet. Look, go out into the garden and play for a bit. I want to talk to Richard and Katy,' said Mrs Cole. Her cheeks were as pink as her slippers. I started to sweat with fear and embarrassment.

'I'm watching "Grange Hill"! Oh Mum, don't be mean,' Wendy wailed, as Mrs Cole reached over and switched the television off.

The room was suddenly silent.

'I was watching that. It's my favourite programme. You aren't half mean,' Wendy mumbled. 'I'm going to switch it on again,' she said, her hand darting out, but she obviously didn't quite dare turn the switch.

'Stop being so cheeky. Go on out to play. I'm warning you, Wendy. Out in the garden this minute. Look, get yourself an ice lolly from the freezer.'

Wendy's protests became more half-hearted and she let Mrs Cole scoop her from the room. I stared helplessly at Richard. He put his hand over mine and squeezed it fiercely. Mrs Cole closed the lounge door and stood facing us, her hands on her hips.

'Now, what is all this? Come on, out with it,' she said sharply. Her lips twitched sideways with distaste as she looked at me. 'Are you going to have a baby?'

'No, I am not!' If it hadn't been for Richard's commonsense and ingenuity I might well have been pregnant, but I resented the accusation bitterly all the same.

Richard jumped up and faced his mother.

'Don't you dare talk to her like that!'

His fists were clenched, his feet bouncing in their trainers. Mrs Cole was the same height as him. She thrust her chest out aggressively, her chin jabbing the air. It looked as if they were about to start sparring.

'Katy and I are in love. Don't you dare take that attitude. Of course she's not having a baby. You apologise to her, Mum! I won't have you saying stuff like that.'

'All right, all right. Calm down, Richard. There's no need to get in such a state,' she said, taken aback. 'Look, let's all sit down and talk this over sensibly.'

She sat down in her armchair and reached for her handbag. She found cigarettes and a dainty pink enamel lighter. She had difficulty working it, flicking it again and again. Her nails were long and carefully manicured. I clenched my own ragged fingers into my palms.

'Give it here, Mum,' said Richard irritably, taking the lighter from her and producing a flame first time. Her hand cupped his as he lit her cigarette. I hated their closeness. She behaved like a rival girl-friend, not his mother.

'Now,' she said, drawing heavily on the cigarette. 'Do you want one, Richard?' As he took one she hesitated and held the packet in my direction. 'Do you?'

I shook my head.

'Now,' she repeated. 'What's all this about? Why the sudden rush of events? We've been kept in the dark about Katy for weeks and then suddenly here she is, and you're asking if she can stay here and saying that you're actually engaged. You must admit, it is a bit sudden, isn't it? And what's all this about Katy's father?'

'He's furious with her. They had a terrible row and he kept hitting her. I can't let her go home to face more of that. I'm not having him beating her up.'

'He didn't really beat me, Richard.'

'You're terrified of him, you know you are. It's ridiculous, Mum, Katy's hardly ever allowed to go out and she's been frightened all this time of her Dad finding out that we're seeing each other. She always said he'd go berserk and now he has.'

Mrs Cole was watching me carefully.

'Did your father hit you, Katy?'

181

'Well, sort of. But it was because of my O levels. That's what started it all. I didn't do as well as he'd hoped and – '

'Yes, that proves he's completely round the twist. She did marvellously, she passed nine, and she got an A, that's the best grade of all, in five of them. And yet her Dad acted as if it was the end of the world, can you believe it?'

'No, you see, everyone thought I'd – it's difficult to explain, but – '

'So you came running round to Richard after this row with your father, right?' said Mrs Cole. 'And what exactly have you two been planning, eh?'

'We thought that Katy could stay here for a bit. And then – well, she wants to get a job, so she could pay you for her board, and then I'd put in extra out of my wages too,' said Richard.

'What do you mean, a job? She'll be going back to school in a couple of weeks.'

'No, she doesn't want to. She's fed up with it all. She's been in such a state over these exams, because everyone's pushed her so hard.'

'So you're giving up school too, are you?' said Mrs Cole, turning back to me. 'Yet you go to Lady Margaret Whatsit's, don't you? Their girls don't generally leave at sixteen. You *are* sixteen, aren't you?'

'Well, not until next January,' I mumbled. 'I was put up a year.'

'Then what's all this talk about getting a job?' Mrs Cole said scornfully. 'Come on, you two! She can't work, not if she's only fifteen.'

'Well, all right, she'll have to go back to school, but she could still stay here, couldn't she? I said *I'll* pay for her board,' said Richard. 'And then when she's a bit older we're going to get married and we'll get a place of our own.'

'You're going to do all this on your wages, are you? Pay board for two people *and* save up for a place of your own?' said Mrs Cole. 'Grow up, Richard!'

But Richard seemed to be growing down. He puffed repeatedly on his cigarette, his face screwed up with despair.

'We'll manage, I tell you,' he said.

'I'd better go home.'

'No! You're staying,' said Richard thickly.

182

He bent his head. Two tears suddenly spurted down his cheeks. He stubbed his cigarette out furiously and sniffed. There was a terrible pause.

'Well, anyway, let's say Katy's staying for supper. So that means I haven't got enough beefburgers and I could do with some more rolls too. And a pound of tomatoes as we had salad at lunch. So you'd better run down to the shop on the corner before it shuts, Richard. Take my purse. Here, love.' She pressed it into his hand so that he could get out of the room quickly. But it wasn't just concern for her son's dignity. She wanted to get me on my own.

As soon as the door slammed she turned to me.

'What are you playing at, eh?' she said.

'I don't know what you mean.'

'Come on, Katy. Let's have this out once and for all. Can't you see what you're doing to Richard? I can't bear it, seeing my lad in tears like that.'

She dabbed at her own eyes with a clean pink tissue and then dropped it in the floral waste-paper basket, scarcely used. I didn't reply to her, staring determinedly at the patterns on the carpet. There were fuzzy purple rings and sudden spirals of crimson. Perhaps they were supposed to be planets. I projected myself into their weird woolly world, flying round the rings and through the spirals, light years away from Mrs Cole and her cold questions.

'Katy! I'm talking to you. You've knocked Richard sideways, don't you realise? He's got such a big heart and he's so sensitive and caring. I always knew he'd fall hard. He was full of you right from the first time he met you. He bored the pants off us all with his Katy this and Katy that.'

I somersaulted through the red atmosphere, stepping from one planet to another, determined not to listen.

'But you couldn't be content just to have him adoring you, could you? Oh no, you had to start changing him. He'd start clapping his hand over his mouth because Miss Snobby Snootikins didn't approve of some harmless expression, and then we had all this fuss fuss fuss over his clothes. Not good enough for you, were they?'

Her voice was getting louder. I couldn't help hearing her.

'Then you got him going to all sorts of silly places, and he even started on about going to evening classes in History, for God's sake. History! What earthly good is that to him? And then he disrupted the whole routine of the household by going on the night-shift at the works. You've no idea what a nuisance it is, two men working one shift and one another. There was no need for him to work nights, not yet, and because he's been so awkward he's missed out on a chance of working this new machine they've got in. The other apprentice has jumped in instead and yet he started six months after Richard. His Dad told him he'd miss out but he wouldn't listen.'

'I didn't know any of this,' I said sulkily.

'No, because you're not really interested, are you? You don't love Richard, do you?'

'I do.'

'Not properly. Not *love*. Because if you really loved him you'd not keep on at him so. You've been making his life a misery, haven't you? We can always tell when you've been having a go at him. The poor kid mopes around here with his tail between his legs, and we just can't get through to him. We've always been such a close, happy family. We didn't have any of this trouble with Mick. His Barbara fitted into the family straight away and now I look on her practically as my own daughter. But you haven't made any effort. You thought you were too good to come to tea with us, didn't you?'

'No! I couldn't. My father – '

'You seem to be using your father as an excuse an awful lot of the time. Well, you mightn't get on well with your family, but Richard was always a lovely boy to have around until you started changing him. He's always been so good with Wendy, and yet this summer he's hardly spent any time with her and it's really affected her, she's gone back to being all whiny and clinging – '

'It's not my fault that your daughter doesn't know how to behave,' I said furiously.

I was more angry with Richard than his mother. I was appalled at all the things he'd told his family. How could he want to share me with them? I had kept him my own special secret. Nicola knew about him, but I'd scarcely told her anything.

'Don't you start giving me your lip, Madam,' said Mrs Cole.

184

'I've been watching you this afternoon. I've seen the way you've turned your nose up at me. And Wendy. And this room. I've seen that face you pull, that unpleasant little sneer. Yes, you might well look ashamed! But I don't care what you think of us. All that matters is that you care about Richard. But you *don't*. You look at him in the same snobby little way. You don't look at him and think he's wonderful, do you? When he looks at you I can see his whole guts are melting, God help him. But not you. You're just using him, aren't you? He's helping you get through a sticky patch in your life. But what are you going to do with him when you've got yourself sorted out and you've stopped having your silly little tantrums about your school exams? Well?'

I didn't answer her. There was no point. We both knew she was right. I stared at the carpet in silence, and then I deliberately overfocused so that my eyes blurred and watered. Once I'd got started off I could cry easily. So I cried and after several very long minutes she passed me a wad of pink tissues and awkwardly patted my hands.

'There now. I suppose I was a bit hard on you. It's just that Richard's my son and of course I have to take his side. But there's no need to take on so. I dare say it'll all come right in the end. You're staying for supper and I suppose you might as well stay the night now you're here – although you can't stay for good, you do understand, don't you? Come on, dry your eyes. Richard will be back in a minute.'

Wendy had her nose pressed hard against the window, watching us wide-eyed. Mrs Cole let her in and and I scrubbed at my face and when Richard got back we were all three playing 'Happy Families'. The irony escaped him. His face lit up when he saw us. It made me want to cry properly.

So I stayed and had supper at the Coles' and I met Mr Cole and Michael Cole. They were both bigger, broader, beefier versions of Richard. They were very nice to me in their own way, calling me K-K-K-Katy like the song, and Curlynob because of my hair and Brainbox when they heard how many O levels I'd passed. I kept a smile stretched tightly across my face, hating them because I knew that Richard would grow up to be just like them.

When Mrs Cole said I was staying the night there were a lot

185

of mildly ribald remarks, while Richard blushed painfully and smiled like me. Wendy seemed surprisingly keen on the idea of my sharing her bedroom and rushed round importantly finding me pillows and nighties and towels.

'But you'll have to phone your parents first, Katy,' Mrs Cole said firmly. 'I want you to get their permission.'

'Oh please, I don't want to.'

'I can't help that, dear, I'm saying you've got to.' She frowned at me. 'They do know you're here, don't they?'

'Well –'

'Good God, your mother must be worrying herself silly. Phone straight away.'

I looked at Richard for help but he nodded.

'You'd better phone, Katy. I mean, it's only fair on your Mum. Go on. Speak to her, not your Dad. Don't worry, it'll be all right. Look, shall I phone for you?'

But I dialled myself and waited, my heart thudding.

'Yes?' Dad barked, so loudly that it was as if he was crouching in the receiver, ready to spring at me.

'Oh Dad, I'm –'

'How dare you! We've been considering going to the police. Where are you? You're to get yourselves home this minute or by God I'll –'

'I'm sorry, Dad –'

'I'll give you bloody sorry! The pair of you deserve a damn good hiding and I've a mind to give it you too, one after the other. Now come home, do you hear me? Both of you.'

'I – Dad, do you want Richard to come too?'

'What? That boy? Of course I bloody don't! You're never to go near him again. If I get my hands on him I'll –'

'Then what do you mean, both of you?'

'What? Stop messing me about. You and Nicola.'

'Nicola?'

'Wash your ears out, girl. *Nicola*. She's with you, isn't she?'

And that was when we realised Nicola was missing.

Chapter 20

But I was sure I knew where she'd be.

'She'll be at our house, Richard. I'm sure she's followed us there sometimes. She knows which one it is. She'll be hiding there, I bet you anything.'

'What do you mean, your house?' Mrs Cole said sharply.

'It's just a place we've been to once or twice, Mum,' Richard said. 'I'd better go with Katy to look for Nicola.'

'And you say she's gone missing? How old is she? Thirteen? And how long has she been missing for?'

'I don't really know,' I said. 'She went out early this morning.' I shook my head, not wanting to think about Nicola rushing out, her face distorted with crying. I saw the torn limbs of the paper people, the scurf from the snowstorm . . ..

'But she'll be all right,' I said quickly. 'I mean, she's not really *missing*. She often goes off for the day like this. She'll just be staying out this late to show us. We had a row and Nicola was upset . . . but she'll be all right.'

I kept on saying it, as if repeating it often enough would make it true. I thanked Mrs Cole for having me and said goodbye to Mr Cole and Michael and Wendy – who moaned and muttered because it was now obvious that I wasn't spending the night with the Coles after all.

I took Richard's hand and we walked quickly to our house. We were running hard by the time we'd got to the right street.

'But I *know* she'll be there. I know Nicola. I think she's been there sometimes before. She'll be there, Richard, you'll see,' I gasped, pulling my hand away so that I could run even faster.

I fell in the garden, catching my foot in the brambles and landing painfully on my hands and knees. I scraped half the skin off my palms and tore a hole in my jeans but I was up again before Richard got to me. I scrambled through the window, cutting my hand again on the jagged glass, almost glad of the fresh pain. Once, twice. I deliberately banged into the sagging banister, knocking my elbow so hard I had to clutch it to my side for a moment, my eyes squeezed shut to try to bear it. Three hurts, three chances, so Nicola had to be there.

'Nic! Nic! Nicola!' I called although I hated hearing the reediness of my voice in the derelict house. I burst into every room, calling again and again. I looked under the rugs although they were folded flat. I peered behind the shell of the sofa. I even went into the reeking toilet and looked round dementedly, although there was nowhere Nicola could possibly be hiding.

'She's not here, Katy,' said Richard.

'She's got to be! Look, maybe she's in the garden. We didn't search there properly. She'll be tucked up under one of those bushes, I bet you. Come on, let's look.'

'We'd have seen her, Katy,' said Richard, but he followed me helplessly while I staggered backwards and forwards in the wilderness of the garden, calling and calling until my voice grew hoarse.

I gave up in the end and stood biting my lip, my sore hands pressed against my eyes, trying to keep the tears inside. Richard put his arms round me but I pulled away from him violently. I didn't want to be comforted.

'She's probably turned up at your house by now,' said Richard. 'Come on. We've got to get you home anyway. Don't forget, your parents are worrying about you too. Don't be afraid. I'm coming with you and I'm not going to let your father lay a hand on you.'

His voice seemed to be coming from a long way away, the other side of the garden, although we were standing so close we were touching. But what he said made some sort of sense, so I let him hold my hand again and pull me away home. He talked to me on the way, but I made his voice grow fainter until I could only hear a vague mumble. I listened to my own voice inside my head. LET NICOLA BE ALL RIGHT. LET NICOLA BE ALL RIGHT. LET NICOLA BE ALL RIGHT.

Of course she was going to be all right. Why was I getting in such a state? She *did* often stay out all day by herself. She'd always come home around four before, but that was when she was supposed to be at school. She'd just decided to stay out later to make a point. To show she didn't care. To make *us* care. She wasn't at our house but she'd obviously found some other place. Or she could just be walking around. It was still light and it was quite warm, even though I couldn't stop shivering. No, Richard was right, she'd be back at home, and Dad would be yelling at her and Mum would be crying, but when I walked in they'd both turn on me and Nicola would be all right.

But she wasn't at home. Mum and Dad both came to the top of the stairs when they heard me come in the side-door.

'I thought I told you to come back straight away!' Dad yelled. He glared ferociously at Richard. 'And tell that lad to make himself scarce before I knock him into next week.' But he sounded like a bad actor. There was no real threat in his voice. He didn't do anything when Richard came up the stairs with me. He barely seemed to notice him.

'You haven't been with Nicola, Katherine?' Mum said, taking hold of my hands. 'You don't have any idea where she is?'

'She'll be back any minute, Mum. She'll be all right,' I gabbled. 'She's just doing it because – well, you know. This morning.'

'Where have you been then, Katherine?' Dad said to me. 'You do realise, I've been round and round the bally town looking for you. I didn't know what to think. You deserve a good hiding, you wicked girl. I've a good mind to give it you, teach you a lesson once and for all.'

He took several shuffling steps towards me but even Richard realised he didn't mean it. Dad took hold of me suddenly by the shoulder. His eyes were bloodshot and silted up at the corners. He smelt sour. He clutched at my shoulder, digging his fingers in, uncertain whether to shake me or hug me.

'You're too thin. Too skinny by half. Feel, there's no flesh on her at all,' he said to Mum.

She looked at me, trying to focus.

'Do you want your tea?' she said slowly. 'It's still in the oven. I did Toad in the Hole. It's probably frizzled up by now, but I could do you an egg or something.'

'No, Mum, I've already eaten.'

'I knew you'd be all right, Katherine,' said Mum. 'You can

look after yourself. You've been running wild all summer anyway. But Nicola – '

'She'll be all right, Mum. She's a lot more independent than you think. She's just staying out because she's upset.'

'But she wouldn't stay out this late. Not unless. . .. She wouldn't worry me. She'd phone at the very least. You phoned. Katherine, are you sure you haven't got any idea at all where she can be?'

'I was sure I knew, but she's not at this place where I thought she'd be. I don't know, Mum.' I went and stood by the china cabinet, trying to think. 'She said she goes down by the river sometimes.'

Mum gasped, hands flying to her massive chest.

'She won't have fallen *in*, Mum, she's not a baby.'

'But there's always funny types hanging round by the river.'

'No there aren't. Anyway, she probably hasn't been anywhere near there. There's no need to get into such a panic. It's not really late. I mean, lots of girls Nicola's age, even younger, they stay out for hours and hours.'

'Not all day too. She hasn't had her lunch or her tea. Something terrible's happened, I just know it has. She'd never stay out all day long, never. While the two of you were missing I kept telling myself you might have met up, and that Nicola would be all right if she was with you, and that you were both just egging each other on. Your Dad kept saying that was what had happened. We guessed you'd be with – ' Mum nodded in Richard's direction. 'Your Dad kept on that Nicola was with you. But now – '

Tears spilled down Mum's face, glistening on her cheeks like sweat. She looked so awful when she cried. I went to her and tried to hold her, shielding her, mostly because I couldn't bear Richard to watch her like that.

'Turn off those bally waterworks, that's no help,' Dad barked. 'Look, I keep telling you, woman, she'll be all right. This one's turned up safe and sound, hasn't she? Nicola will too. And by God she'll be for it then, getting us all into this state.' He was starting to build up momentum, sounding more his old self. He whirled round to me and saw that my hand was still lying limply in Richard's. Dad slapped at our hands ineffectually, his face puckered. 'Leave go of her, will you? I

190

don't know why you're hanging round here, laddie, you're not wanted. Get yourself home.'

'Shall I go and look down by the river, see if I can see Nicola, if you really think there's a chance she might be there, Katy?' Richard said to me.

'Katy! Her name's Katherine, although it's no business of yours. She's having nothing more to do with you. You've turned my daughter into a deceitful little liar and she's all but wrecked her Oxbridge chances on your behalf.'

'Dad, I didn't even *know* Richard when I sat my O levels,' I said, but it didn't really matter now. 'I'll come with you, Richard.'

'Oh no you won't. You're staying put, my lady. *I'll* go out looking for her,' said Dad, buttoning up his jacket.

'I think we ought to phone the police,' said Mum. She said it so quietly that for a moment we all pretended we hadn't heard. Then Dad hissed with exasperation.

'You can't go to the police just because Nicola's playing us up like this. They've got more to do than look for naughty schoolgirls. Now, I'm going out. Down by the river you say, Katherine?'

'Or she goes round the town sometimes, only all the shops will be shut, so – Dad, I don't *know.*'

'Fat lot of help you are,' Dad snapped, pushing past me. 'You see to your mother then. Don't you dare set a foot out of the house. And send lover-boy here packing, I'm telling you.'

He barged out of the room. Mum shook her head. She started to sit down, missed the edge of the chair, and went on sitting until she was on the carpet. She did it slowly, her skirts billowing out round her, her dreadful underwear showing.

'Mum! Get up.' I went to her and pulled at her arm.

Mum didn't seem to notice. 'I've been on and on at him to phone the police, but he won't. I know something's happened to her. I know it has. She wouldn't stay out this late. It'll be getting dark soon and she's terrified of the dark. She'd have been back hours ago if she could.'

'Look Mum, you don't know Nicola. Don't say anything to Dad, but this last term she's been staying away from school a lot. Truly she has. She's used to wandering about on her own, she's been doing it for a while. All day long, Mum, honestly.'

191

'Don't give me that. That's something you'd do, not Nicola.'

'I swear it, Mum. Oh do get up. She was being teased by the other girls so she played truant. I met her out, when she should have been in school. Richard, if you get her other arm –'

'Leave me be!' Mum shrieked, not even letting me pull her skirt down decently. 'You mean you knew, and you didn't tell me?'

'I didn't want to get her into trouble. You know how Dad would have reacted. I'm sorry, I know I should have said, but I never thought – She will be all right though, you'll see. She's not doing it to get at you, it's me, because I've been so hateful to her.' I was crying too.

Richard stood helplessly, staring from Mum to me, muttering that he was sure Nicola would turn up quickly, as right as rain.

It got darker and darker in the room but nobody bothered to turn on the light. We couldn't see at all when we heard the door downstairs. We stiffened into statues, but there were only Dad's slow footsteps on the stairs. When he came into the room he looked exhausted, his hair in damp strands across his head, his jacket streaked, his shoes muddy.

'It's started raining.' He paused. 'There's no sign of her,' he said, almost matter-of-fact.

'I'm going to phone the police,' said Mum, and this time he didn't argue with her.

She heaved herself to her feet while Richard politely averted his eyes.

'Give it here,' said Dad, reaching for the receiver, but Mum ignored him.

She dialled the number and then spoke in a surprisingly calm way to the duty officer at the police station. She gave Nicola's name and age, said she was wearing a white T-shirt, a pink and white cotton skirt, a pale blue knitted cardigan, white socks and white plimsolls. She said she had gone out of the house at half past nine this morning and hadn't been seen since. She'd never stayed out in the evening before.

Ten minutes later the police arrived, a man and a woman. They were both surprisingly young, with very short haircuts and pink, eager faces, but their uniform was frightening all the

192

same. Mum shook as she led them into the sitting-room and asked if they'd like a cup of tea.

'So your daughter's been missing about twelve hours now?' said the policeman, still standing, although Mum had twice asked him to sit down.

Oh God. It sounded so awful.

'We didn't *know* she was missing though, not during the day. We thought she was just out playing,' said Dad. 'That's why we didn't get in touch with you, sir. We didn't want to waste your time, you see. We thought she'd just decided to stay out late. But then, well, it got later and later. I've been out looking for her, I've been round the whole town twice, down by the river, everywhere. I don't know where she could have got to. I mean, she doesn't normally run wild, sir. We've done our best to bring her up properly.' I couldn't bear the way he kept calling him sir. He was fawning, trying to get the young policeman to absolve him from blame.

'Do you mind if we have a quick look over the premises, sir?' said the policeman. The crisp way he said sir made it plain to Dad that he'd got the procedure wrong.

'Be my guest – officer,' he said, gesturing uneasily.

'You want to look round?' said Mum worriedly, coming in with an empty teapot. 'I'm afraid it's not very tidy. I was a bit upset today so I never got round to the housework. I'm not even sure the girls' beds are made.'

'Don't you worry, Mrs Petworthy,' said the policewoman kindly. 'I'm sure my bed isn't made either. It's just to check that Nicola isn't hiding anywhere. Would you like me to make the tea for you? Okay, Dave?'

Dave the policeman slipped away to search. Dad shook his head in bewilderment and then followed him.

'I don't get this, officer,' he said, no longer deferential. 'Nicola went *out*, her mother saw her go out.'

'Yes, I know, sir, but she might have crept back without you hearing her. She might be hiding just now, scared of getting into trouble.'

'She's no reason to be scared. Are you saying she's scared of me?'

'No, of course not, sir, it's just – '

'And why would she hide? She's thirteen years old, not

three, and she's damn near as tall as you are. She's a bit big for this hiding caper.'

'It's simply a routine search, sir,' the policeman said, unruffled. 'You'd be surprised the number of missing children who are found hiding in their own houses.'

Their voices got fainter as they went upstairs. The policewoman came back carrying a tray of teacups. Mum came in and started to pour. Then she stopped, spilling tea.

'We're using the wrong china,' she said. 'This is just the old chipped set. Katherine, can you – '

'Oh Mum, as if it matters. Go on pouring.'

I turned to the policewoman. Little wisps of hair stuck out from underneath her severe cap. She wasn't wearing any make-up, not even powder. I could see all the blackheads on her nose, like a sprinkling of pepper.

'When are you going to start searching for my sister?' I said aggressively.

'Don't worry, love, her description's been circulated already and everyone's looking out for her. We're doing our best,' she said, smiling at me. She had very white, even teeth. She didn't look nearly so bad when she smiled.

'Come here, Katy,' said Richard, trying to hold me.

I'd forgotten he was even there. So had Mum. There weren't enough teacups.

'Who are you then, love?' said the policewoman.

'Richard Cole. I'm Katy's boy-friend.'

'I'll get you a cup,' Mum said, fumbling up her vast sleeve for her sodden handkerchief.

'No, really, I don't want any tea. Oh Katy.' He held on to me as if his clasp could somehow help me.

'You'd better go home, Richard,' I said. 'Oh God, I'd forgotten, you've got to go to work. I'm sorry, you'll be exhausted.'

'I'm fine,' Richard insisted, although now I noticed the grey smudges under his eyes. 'Look, I could stay off work if you like. Wouldn't you sooner I stayed, Katy?'

'There's no point,' I said – and then realised I'd hurt him. But I couldn't think of a way of smoothing things over. I was concentrating too hard on Nicola to want to be bothered with him.

'All right, I'll go then,' he said huffily. 'I'll ring the minute I get in from work tomorrow morning just to check Nicola's turned up. But don't worry, she'll be all right, you'll see.'

He kissed my cheek, patted Mum's arm, and went. Mum stared after him vaguely.

'He seems a nice boy,' she muttered.

'Does Nicola have a boy-friend?' the policewoman asked.

She was looking at me but I didn't say anything.

Mum was looking puzzled. 'Nicola's only thirteen.'

'Yes, but – '

'Nicola's not a precocious girl. She's young for her age.'

'Tell me about Nicola's girl-friends then.'

'Well, I don't really know that she has many. She's never really – ' Mum looked at me worriedly. 'Would you say she's got any special friends, Katherine?'

I shook my head. 'She's rather an odd one out.'

'What about at school? How does she get on there?'

'All right,' said Mum. 'She's quite good at her lessons. Not startling, like this one, but she tries her hardest.'

'And she's happy there? And at home?'

'Oh yes,' said Mum, nodding in emphasis.

'You said you were upset this morning, Mrs Petworthy.'

'Did I?' said Mum, looking startled. 'Would you like a biscuit? I'm sorry, I didn't – there's custard creams or I could get some KitKats from the shop?'

'No, I'm fine, thanks. Yes, something happened this morning? Did you and Nicola have a little row?'

'Oh no. Nicola and I, we get on well. No, this morning, well, that was different. That was to do with Katherine.'

The policewoman stared at me. She waited, asking general questions, until the policeman came back with Dad.

'I've left the girls' bedroom for you, Meg,' he said.

She nodded and then turned to me. 'Come and show me your bedroom, Katherine, there's a dear.'

I didn't want to go in our bedroom. I saw the broken snowstorm straight away, lying against the skirting-board. I saw the remnants of our Paper People. I saw Nicola's socks and knickers from yesterday in grubby little balls beside her bed. I saw Sniffle, Woffle, and Muffle and I couldn't bear it.

'Do you think something's happened to her?' I whispered, wiping my eyes on a corner of the sheet.

'I'm sure we'll find her safe and sound. Did she have any money saved that she might have taken with her?'

'No, none.'

'And what about her clothes? Are any missing? Coat, jeans, party clothes?' said the policewoman, opening the wardrobe.

'She wouldn't have had time to take anything. She just rushed out.'

'Why?'

I sat down on the end of Nicola's bed, clutching Muffle.

'Because I was hateful to her. I said dreadful things. I've been horrible to her all these holidays and now – and now. . . .'
I was sobbing so hard that I couldn't talk any more. I pressed my face into Muffle's matted fur.

She put her arm round my shoulders.

'Don't blame yourself, my love. All sisters have rows. I've said terrible things to my sister so many times I've lost count. Now, where do *you* think she went?'

'I don't know. There's this derelict house I go to with Richard sometimes, I thought she might be there, and we went and searched and searched, but she wasn't there.'

'And you're sure too that Nicola hasn't a boy-friend? You looked a bit funny when I was talking to your Mum. I won't say anything to her, I promise. But do you know of *anyone* Nicola might have gone to? She's never mentioned any boy to you?'

I hesitated, snuffling into Muffle. 'Well, she's been going on about this boy – but she's just made him up, I know she has. He's not a real person, he's just imaginary, only Nicola gets so carried away sometimes she can't seem to tell the difference.'

'What's his name?'

'Charles Christmas. I mean, it's a silly made-up name for a start. And she pretended he gave her a book and took her on all sorts of outings, but he didn't really, it was just Nicola trying to get back at me, because I kept showing off about Richard.'

'You don't know where he's supposed to live?'

'He doesn't live anywhere, she made him up,' I said.

'But you're not one hundred per cent sure? We'd better check anyway, just to see if there really is a Charles Christmas living in the area.'

She called the station on her radio and then listened, frowning. I heard the voice at the other end of the radio too.

196

'Yes, I know Charles Christmas. He's one of the town's real characters. He's a bloke in his fifties who hangs around the river most days. Tuppence short of a shilling after some sort of breakdown, but he talks very posh. What's he been up to, then?'

Chapter 21

They went off to interview Charles Christmas. The police-woman saw I'd heard and grew uncomfortable.

'Don't worry so, lovey. We've got to check him out, but he's probably nothing to do with your sister. And anyway, he sounds perfectly harmless.'

But he grew monster-like in my mind. I saw him as a slavering beast with thick wet lips like slugs. No, she'd be terrified of someone like that. She knew this Charles Christmas, she'd gone to see him nearly every day, she'd turned him into a friend. So he couldn't look like a monster. She'd called him a gentleman. The policeman said he was very posh. I disguised the monster in a pin-stripe suit. I gave him greying hair, long pale hands with clean finger-nails, a quiet, cultured voice. Nicola would feel safe with a man like that. She'd be flattered by his attention. He'd be a surrogate father, reassuring her, telling her things. She'd take his hand trustingly, amble happily by his side, eat his sweets, go on little outings with him.

Oh God, why hadn't I believed her? I was so sure she was making him up and yet I *knew* Nicola, I knew she couldn't make anything up herself, she always needed me to do it for her. She hadn't invented Charles Christmas. He was real. But she'd képt him hidden away from me because he wasn't a proper boy-friend, he was an old man in his fifties, a man as old as Dad.

Could he really have just a fatherly interest in Nicola? She wasn't cute and cuddly. She was a great gawky girl, and so painfully gullible. Did she run straight to Charles Christmas today and tell him how hateful I'd been? Did he sit her on his lap and let her sob? And then did he take her somewhere? Somewhere new, somewhere secret? She'd have trotted along willingly enough. But then, when they were hidden away in the secret place, did he pounce? I saw his clean finger-nails fumbling, his cultured voice thickening with terrible desire . . ..

She'd be helpless. I thought of Mr Tremble and how he frightened Nicola, even though he was only a little Paper Person. He was littered over our bedroom lino now, half a head here, a trouser leg there.

I suddenly saw scattered segments of Nicola lying on some lonely river bank: an arm, still wearing its T-shirt sleeve, a fat, pink leg with a grubby, white sock, a head . . ..

I rushed for the bathroom but I couldn't make it in time. My beefburger supper and my toasted cheese sandwich lunch ended up on the landing carpet.

'For God's sake!' Dad bellowed in disgust. 'Get yourself over the toilet! As if we haven't got enough bother. Stop it!'

Mum didn't say anything, although she was the one who went for the bucket and cloth and mopped it all up, while I went on retching and sobbing and shaking. When she'd finished and the hall was reeking of Harpic she came and wrapped my dressing-gown round me.

'There now. It's the shock, I know. You'd be better off in bed.'

'No! I can't go to bed while Nicola's . . . Mum, it's my fault. I knew. I knew about this Charles Christmas person. That's where the police have gone, to interview him. He's in his *fifties*, and Nicola's been seeing him, only I didn't believe her, I thought she was making it up. Oh Mum, if I'd said then Dad would have stopped her staying off school and she'd be safe now. And it was my fault she ran off this morning, it was because I said she was stupid and sneaking and pathetic. I was so awful to her and she was so nice to me about my O levels. It's all my fault, isn't it?'

I clung to my mother, burrowing against her warm bulk, desperate for her to wrap her great arms round me and rock me and tell me that it wasn't my fault after all. But she went rigid when I started burbling about Charles Christmas. She pushed me away from her so she could see my face properly.

'What man? Nicola knew a man? *Tell me!*'

So I told her the little that I knew and then Dad came and

199

stood over me and I had to go through it all over again, and then he started shouting and Mum started crying, and I bit down into my cut hands. I tried to chant LET NICOLA BE ALL RIGHT but the words wouldn't come. NICOLA'S DEAD my head tolled relentlessly. NICOLA'S DEAD. NICOLA'S DEAD.

I loved her so much. I couldn't love Dad properly because I was frightened of him and I often despised him. I couldn't love Mum properly because she was weak and I was ashamed of her. I couldn't love Richard properly although I'd pretended so hard that I did. I badly wanted to love him but I couldn't change him and I couldn't love him the way he was. It wasn't just the shameful, stupid reasons, his haircut, his slang, his clothes. It was because he didn't really understand me. He didn't really love me because he didn't know the real me. Dad didn't know me, Mum didn't know me. But Nicola did. I could make Nicola do what I wanted but I could never fool her. She always knew what I was feeling. We often felt the same.

We were almost part of each other, Katherine and Nicola. We had been conspirators until this summer. I remembered the time we broke the teacup and stole another from Woolworth's, the time we both dressed up in Mum's frock and got the giggles and split the seam, the time we pretended Beecham's powder was deadly poison and sprinkled half a packet into Dad's porridge, the time we both wet our knickers and washed them out secretly and cooked them dry in the oven. I remembered *The Railway Children* and *Swallows and Amazons* games and the Beatrix Potter ballets, the Sniffle, Woffle and Muffle saga, the Paper People, the Black and White Island, the Revolving Castle, Hungry Harriet, the Rude Word game. Then I remembered all the times I'd been mean to Nicola, going right back to not letting her share my snowstorm, the little mean, petty things escalating up to my cruelty this summer.

I'm sorry, I wept. I'm *sorry*. You've got to be all right so I can tell you how sorry I am.

Eventually Dad stopped shouting and ordered me to bed, but I wouldn't go. The three of us stayed hunched in the living-room, glancing at the clock every two or three minutes, staring at the silent telephone, lifting our heads whenever a car went by. At twelve o'clock Dad phoned the police and started

200

shouting at them, telling them that he was coming down to the station to sort this pervert out. Give him five minutes alone with this Christmas slime and he'd soon find out what he'd done with his little girl. But the police told Dad they weren't holding anybody. They'd interviewed one gentleman who did apparently know Nicola slightly, but he hadn't seen her for several days.

'They surely don't believe him!' I shouted. 'Have they searched his house? Why aren't they questioning him properly? Why can't they find Nicola? Why? *Why?*' I was screaming. Mum heaved herself up and got hold of me.

'You're getting hysterical. You're worn out, Katherine. Go to bed. There's no point getting yourself in this state. It doesn't help.'

I let her take me upstairs and she tucked me into bed as if I was little. I tried to pull her down to kiss me, but she stepped back quickly.

'Try to sleep now.'

'You blame me, don't you, Mum? You think it's all my fault.'

'It doesn't matter what I think,' said Mum. 'I can't be bothered thinking who's to blame. Now do stop being such a nuisance and go to sleep.'

It was even worse in the room by myself. I lay huddled in a cold ball, my knees up under my chin. I chanted, I prayed, I made ludicrous bargains with God, but all the time I knew I was only talking to myself. I was alone and it was unbearable. After a while I got up and climbed into Nicola's bed. I clutched Muffle, Woffle and Sniffle and held Nicola's nightie against my cheek. It smelt faintly of her, and I cried until her night-dress was wet.

The phone rang at two o'clock. I leapt out of bed and ran downstairs. I could hear Mum saying 'Yes? Yes?' her voice desperate.

I burst into the room. She was standing holding the phone, fully dressed in her crimplene frock, but with her turquoise dressing-gown over the top. Dad was sitting dazed in the armchair. He was in his pyjamas with two old sweaters pulled on over the top and a rumple of bedclothes wrapped round his legs.

'Yes?' said Mum, and then she gasped. She flung her head

201

back. 'She's safe!' she shouted. 'They've got her! Nicola's safe! They're bringing her straight home in a police car. Oh my God, she's safe!'

She thanked the policeman over and over again, and then Dad took the phone from her and started asking questions. Nicola hadn't gone near poor Charles Christmas. (I met him afterwards. He was no sinister sex fiend. He was a gentle, timid man who wore a neatly pressed suit twenty years out of fashion. He lived with his dominating old mother and always walked with his head jerking back over his shoulder, as if he was scared she was following him).

Nicola had hung about the town all day and had ended up in Rowbridge and Turner's at five o'clock. She'd tried on a dress in the changing room and then hidden in a corner behind a rack of new stock. She thought she'd stay locked up in Rowbridge and Turner's all night long, and walk round all the departments and try on every single dress she fancied and play with all the toys and eat some of the cakes and sweets in the food department and then curl up in the great, showy, modern four-poster in Bedding. But she hadn't realised all the lights would be turned off. She stayed crouching where she was, terrified, wishing she was home even though she was sure we all hated her and wouldn't be missing her at all. She fell asleep after a while, and then woke up and panicked. The security guard heard her screaming and came and found her, still crouched behind the clothes rack.

'Silly little idiot,' said Dad.

There was an unexpected catch in his voice, and when he put the phone down I saw his eyes were brimming with tears.

'I'll give her what for when she gets back,' he said, but he reached out and Mum put her arms round him and they embraced. They were dressed comically in a combination of clothes, Mum looking vaster than ever in her dressing-gown while Dad seemed to have shrunk, but there was nothing to scoff or sneer at about the way they held each other.

'Do you think she ran off because of me?' Dad mumbled.

'No, of course not! She was just being naughty. You know what kids are like. Anyway, she's all right now, and that's all that matters,' Mum said tenderly.

It was all that mattered. I sat waiting for Nicola to come

home. My O level results weren't really that important. And I had passed most of them, after all. And got five A's.

The police took exactly seven minutes to bring Nicola home but it seemed the longest seven minutes of my life. Time seemed to expand and contract dementedly. I'd known Richard for seven weeks and yet it seemed no time at all. I wondered if I'd ever see him again.

At last we heard the police car draw up and there was a great confusion of bells ringing and doors opening and lights going on, and then suddenly there was Nicola, her face grimy with tears, her hair hanging over her forehead, her skirt crumpled, my sister Nicola. I rushed at her and threw my arms round her and I felt her arms go round me and we hugged each other and hugged each other and hugged each other.